JAMIE BYROM
MICHAEL RILEY

THE
CRUSADES

HODDER
EDUCATION
AN HACHETTE UK COMPANY

The authors and publisher wish to thank Jonathan Phillips for his advice as academic consultant. All judgements, interpretations and errors remain the responsibility of the authors.

This book uses the long established western convention of using BC and AD for years before and since the birth of Christ. Where neither is shown the date is AD. The equivalent dates using the Islamic calendar can be found on websites such as http://www.muslimphilosophy.com/ip/hijri.htm.

Photo credits

Cover © PV – Fotolia; **p.4** © Epic/Mary Evans Picture Library; **p.11** © GALI TIBBON/ AFP/Getty Images; **p.12** © incamerastock/Alamy; **p.16** © Metin Cenkmen; **p.18** © The Granger Collection, NYC/TopFoto; **p.21** © Daniel Villafruela / http:// commons.wikimedia.org/wiki/File:Abbaye_Ste_Foy_%C3%A0_Conques_ %2806%29_-_Tympan_du_Porche.jpg / http://creativecommons.org/licenses/ by-sa/2.0/deed.en; **p.23** © Musee de la Tapisserie, Bayeux, France/Bridgeman Art Library/Getty Images; **p.26** © International Photobank/Alamy; **p.32** © The Art Gallery Collection/Alamy; **p.35** © The British Library Board (Shelfmark Add. Ch.19829); **p.38** © Ms Or 20 f.138r The Seljuk Sultan Malik-Shah ibn Alp Arslan, miniature from the 'Jami' al-Tawarikh' of Rashid al-Din, c.1307 (vellum), Islamic School, (14th century)/Edinburgh University Library, Scotland/With kind permission of the University of Edinburgh/The Bridgeman Art Library; **p.41** © North Wind Picture Archives/Alamy; **p.53** © The Art Archive/Kharbine-Tapabor; **p.57** © Tim Barker/Lonely Planet Images/Getty Images; **p.59** © Zoonar GmbH/Alamy; **p.61** © 2010 Mary Evans Picture Library; **p.62** © British Library Board/Robana/TopFoto; **p.63** © British Library Board/Robana/TopFoto; **p.64** © Biblewalks.com; **p.68** © Jonathan Phillips; **p.69** © Classic Image/Alamy; **p.70** Cover of Ronnie Ellenblum: Crusader Castles and Modern Histories, 2009 © Cambridge University Press. Reproduced with permission; **p.77** © Ms Fr 5594 f.138 Saint Bernard (c.1090-1153) of Clairvaux preaching the Second Crusade in the presence of King Louis VII (c.1120-80) of France at Vezelay in 1146, from 'Passages faits Outremer' written by Sebastien Mamerot, c.1490 (vellum), French School, (15th century)/Bibliotheque Nationale, Paris, France/The Bridgeman Art Library; **p.78** © Bibliothèque royale de Belgique (MS.467 f63v); **p.82** © Glencairn Museum, Bryn Athyn, Pennsylvania. Photo by Hans Fischer; **p.84** © World History Archive/Alamy; **p.88** © The Art Archive/Alamy; **p.89** © The Art Gallery Collection/ Alamy; **p.90** © CRESWELL ARCHIVE, ASHMOLEAN MUSEUM, OXFORD, neg. EA. CA.5007. IMAGE COURTESY OF SPECIAL COLLECTIONS, FINE ARTS LIBRARY, HARVARD UNIVERSITY; **p.96** © The Print Collector/Alamy; **p.103** © Duby Tal/ Albatross/Alamy; **p.104** © Photos 12/Alamy; **p.111** © akg-images/Erich Lessing; **p.118** © c – Fotolia; **p.119** © 2004 Gardner/TopFoto; **p.120** © Alfredo Dagli Orti/ The Art Archive/Corbis; **p.122** © Photos 12/Alamy; **p.128** © 2006 Prisma V&W/ TopFoto; **p.130** © Jonathan Phillips; **p.132** © NIKOLAY DOYCHINOV/AFP/Getty Images; **p.133** The Mighty King of Chivalry, Richard the Lionheart, illustration from 'A Pageant of Kings' (gouache on paper), Matania, Fortunino (1881–1963)/Private Collection/© Look and Learn/The Bridgeman Art Library; **p.134** © Godfrey (c.1060-1100) enters Jerusalem, illustration from 'Bibliotheque des Croisades' by J-F. Michaud, 1877 (litho), Dore, Gustave (1832-83)/Private Collection/Ken Welsh/ The Bridgeman Art Library.

Text credits

p.48 Christopher Tyerman: from *God's War: a new History of the Crusades* (Allen Lane, 2006); **p.49** Thomas Asbridge: from *The Crusades* (Simon & Schuster, 2010); **p.60** James Brundage: 'Foundation of the Order of Knights Templar' from William of Tyre's *Historia*, translated by James Brundage, from *The Crusades: A Documentary History* (Marquette University Press, 1962); **p.65** Ronnie Ellenblum: 'Map of Frankish rural sites in the Kingdom of Jerusulam' (Cartographer: Tamar Soffer) from *Frankish Rural Settlement in the Latin Kingdom of Jerusalem* (Cambridge University Press, 1998), © Cambridge University Press 1998; **pp.66 & 67** © Cambridge University Press 1998; Usama ibn Munqidh: from *The Book of Contemplation: Islam and the Crusades*, translated by Paul M. Cobb (Penguin Classics, 2008), **p.71** maps from *Crusader Castles and Modern Histories* (Cambridge University Press, 2007); **p.130** Jonathan Phillips: from *Holy Warriors: A Modern History of the Crusades* (Vintage, 2010), copyright © Jonathan Phillips 2009; **pp.133 & 135** Jonathan Riley-Smith: quoted in an article by Charlotte Edwards from *The Telegraph* (18 January, 2004); from 'Truth is the first victim', *The Times* (5 May, 2005).

Maps on pp.50, 81, 92, 95 and 100 are based on relief maps provided by Treehouse Maps.

Every effort has been made to trace all copyright holders, but if any have been inadvertently overlooked, the Publishers will be pleased to make the necessary arrangements at the first opportunity.

The Schools History Project

Set up in 1972 to bring new life to history for students aged 13–16, the Schools History Project continues to play an innovatory role in secondary history education. From the start, SHP aimed to show how good history has an important contribution to make to the education of a young person. It does this by creating courses and materials which both respect the importance of up-to-date, well-researched history and provide enjoyable learning experiences for students.

Since 1978 the Project has been based at Leeds Trinity University. It continues to support, inspire and challenge teachers through the annual conference, regional courses and website: http://www.schoolshistoryproject.org.uk. The Project is also closely involved with government bodies and awarding bodies in the planning of courses for Key Stage 3, GCSE and A level.

For teacher support material for this title, visit www.schoolshistoryproject.org.uk.

Although every effort has been made to ensure that website addresses are correct at time of going to press, Hodder Education cannot be held responsible for the content of any website mentioned in this book. It is sometimes possible to find a relocated web page by typing in the address of the home page for a website in the URL window of your browser.

Hachette UK's policy is to use papers that are natural, renewable and recyclable products and made from wood grown in sustainable forests. The logging and manufacturing processes are expected to conform to the environmental regulations of the country of origin.

Orders: please contact Bookpoint Ltd, 130 Milton Park, Abingdon, Oxon OX14 4SB. Telephone: + 44 (0)1235 827720. Fax: + 44 (0)1235 400454. Lines are open 9.00a.m.–5.00p.m., Monday to Saturday, with a 24-hour message answering service. Visit our website at www.hoddereducation.co.uk.

© Jamie Byrom and Michael Riley 2013

First published in 2013 by
Hodder Education,
an Hachette UK company
338 Euston Road
London NW1 3BH

Impression number	10	9	8	7	6	5	4	3	2	1
Year			2017	2016	2015	2014	2013			

Typeset in ITC Usherwook Book 10pt by DC Graphic Design Ltd, Swanley Village, Kent.
Artwork by Barking Dog
Printed and bound in Italy
A catalogue record for this title is available from the British Library

ISBN 978 1 4441 4451 2

Contents

The world of the Crusades: Europe, the Near East and North Africa

You may need to refer back to this map as you read the rest of this book.

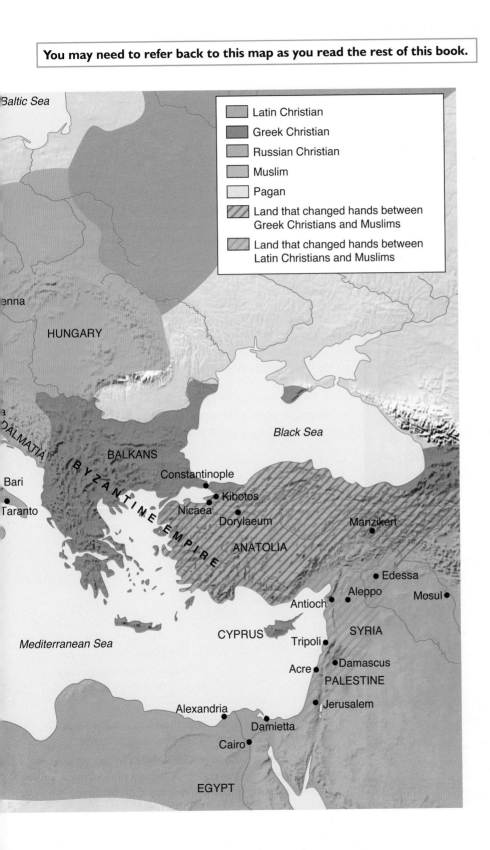

Legend:
- Latin Christian
- Greek Christian
- Russian Christian
- Muslim
- Pagan
- Land that changed hands between Greek Christians and Muslims
- Land that changed hands between Latin Christians and Muslims

Baltic Sea

enna

HUNGARY

DALMATIA

Black Sea

BALKANS

Bari

BYZANTINE EMPIRE

Taranto

Constantinople

Kibotos

Nicaea

Dorylaeum

Manzikert

ANATOLIA

Edessa

Aleppo

Mosul

Antioch

SYRIA

CYPRUS

Tripoli

Mediterranean Sea

Acre

Damascus

PALESTINE

Alexandria

Jerusalem

Damietta

Cairo

EGYPT

1 The Crusades: The essentials

This stained-glass window can be seen at Boulogne in northern France, just across the English Channel. It shows the town's most famous son: Godfrey of Bouillon, often called the first Christian King of Jerusalem. In 1099, he won fame for his part in defeating the Muslim forces that ruled the **Holy Land** where Christ had lived and died. Although the name was never used in Godfrey's time, we now call those wars The Crusades: the wars of the cross.

This window was made in 1900, eight centuries after Godfrey's death. It fits the popular ideal of a crusader. His powerful figure stands fully armed, with his tunic and shield proudly bearing the sign of the cross. His steel sword is held firmly in his grip and he gazes towards the heavens as if looking to God's own kingdom.

A brief summary of Godfrey's story can help us to enter the world of the first crusaders. It was very different in many ways from the world we know today.

> Words in bold (such as Holy Land above) are defined in the glossary on pages 138 and 139.

◁ Duke Godfrey of Bouillon as shown in a stained-glass window at Boulogne sur Mer in northern France.

The window was made in 1899–1900 almost certainly to commemorate the eighth centenary of Godfrey's part in capturing Jerusalem at the end of the First Crusade.

Godfrey was born around 1060 into a wealthy and important noble family that held lands along the borders of what we would now call France, Belgium and Germany. In his day those modern nation states did not exist. The map on pages 2 and 3 shows the world into which Godfrey was born. To help you make sense of his story and to become familiar with some landmarks of the Crusades, locate these places on the map:

- Boulogne, on the north coast of France, where Godfrey was born.

- Bouillon, where he owned his lands, about 100 miles away.

- France, made up of people collectively known as 'The Franks'.

- The **German Empire**, made up of various duchies and kingdoms (including Godfrey's lands at Bouillon).

- The western or 'Latin' Christian lands.

- The eastern or 'Greek' Christian lands which included …
  - The **Byzantine Empire**. (This was the name given to the Roman Empire, which continued in the east long after the western half broke up around AD480.)
  - Constantinople at the southern point of the Black Sea where Europe and Asia were divided by a narrow stretch of sea. This was the magnificent capital city of the Byzantine Empire.

- Jerusalem, over 2500 miles south-east of Boulogne, deep in Muslim-held lands. This is where Godfrey fought, ruled … and then died in AD1100.

Until 1095, Godfrey lived as a minor nobleman with little influence outside his own lands. Then, in that year, Pope Urban II, the leader of the **Latin Church**, called upon western Christians to fight on behalf of their fellow Christians in the Holy Land. The Pope declared that the Christians who lived there were suffering at the hands of their Muslim rulers.

Godfrey answered the Pope's call. He gave up much of his land to raise funds and gathered an army of **knights** and foot soldiers. In August 1096, these first 'crusaders' set off across Europe towards the Holy Land, with the cross of Christ sewn onto their tunics. In the summer of 1096 the different crusader armies gathered at Constantinople, the capital of the Byzantine Empire. They may have numbered 50,000.

Over the next three years this 'army of God' struggled towards Jerusalem, both inflicting and suffering the horrors of war. (Godfrey once ordered that twenty Muslim enemies be blinded to prevent them fighting again.) Along the way, the crusaders experienced disease, famine and death. When horses died, proud knights rode on the backs of cattle. Thousands perished or turned back. About 14,000 reached Jerusalem in June 1099.

On 15 July Godfrey and a group of his knights were the first to climb over the city's high walls, opening the way for the others to follow. This led to a dreadful slaughter of the Muslims and Jews of Jerusalem. Godfrey made his way to the Church of the **Holy Sepulchre**, built on the very place where he believed Christ had risen from the dead. He took off his armour, entered the church and prayed as the bloodshed continued in the streets.

Days later, the crusaders chose the ruler of the new kingdom of Jerusalem. Godfrey accepted the role – but most sources say that he refused the title of 'King', insisting that he would not wear a crown of gold where Christ had worn a crown of thorns.

He died just a year later and was buried in the Church of the Holy Sepulchre. He died believing that his sinful soul would find a place in heaven, not despite his part in the brutal Holy War, but because of it.

This really was a very different age from our own.

The Crusades: 1095–1291

In any study of history it helps to grasp the 'big picture' before getting into the more complex details. You have already met Godfrey of Bouillon. On these two pages we use the true stories of six more individuals to shed light on important times and places in the 200-year history of the Crusades. Follow the stories anticlockwise.

Story 1: Pope Urban II in Clermont – 1095

In November 1095, on a hillside at Clermont in France, Pope Urban II addressed a large gathering. He called on western Christians to take up arms and to travel east to fight against a fierce group of Muslims called the **Seljuk Turks**. These Seljuks had taken land from the Christian Byzantine Empire and, he claimed, they were persecuting Christians and stopping them from visiting the holy city of Jerusalem where Christ had been crucified. Urban II promised that anyone who fought to free Jerusalem from Muslim control would be sure of a place in heaven.

Urban's message spread rapidly and powerfully. Thousands of western Christians joined the 'army of God' and set off on their Holy War. Some, like Godfrey of Bouillon, reached Jerusalem and took the city in July 1099. But Pope Urban II never knew of their success. He died far away in Rome just days after the crusaders' victory.

Story 2: Ibn Munqidh in Damascus – 1143

After taking Jerusalem in 1099, most crusaders returned to Europe but others stayed in the east to guard the city of Jerusalem and the **crusader states** they established along the coast. They lived alongside the Muslims they had conquered. Usama ibn Munqidh was a writer, soldier and diplomat who lived and worked in the city of Damascus in the 1140s. He wrote about the crusader Christians whom he, like all other Muslims, called **Franks**. With some he was on friendly terms, but he made clear his resentment at the arrival of the Franks and his belief that their rule over Muslims was not deserved. He was not the only Muslim with these thoughts and the middle of the twelfth century saw the first real stirrings of a Muslim fight-back.

Story 3: Queen Eleanor of Aquitaine in Sicily – 1149

In 1144 the Muslims recaptured the crusader lands around Edessa and massacred the Christians who lived there. A Second Crusade led by the kings of Germany and France set off for the east. The king of France, Louis VII, was accompanied on crusade by his wife, Queen Eleanor of Aquitaine who was as committed to crusading as any man.

But this Second Crusade was a disaster. Louis, Eleanor and their armies, like those of the German king, struggled to reach the Holy Land and were driven back almost immediately by the Muslim forces. As Eleanor sailed home to France, her ship, like the Crusade that had just failed, was blown off course. When it eventually reached Palermo in Sicily, Eleanor learned how the Crusade's failure had been greeted by a sense of shock and shame in Europe. Some even blamed the defeat on the amount of luggage the army had been carrying for Eleanor and her ladies-in-waiting! Crusading did not guarantee glory.

Story 6: Baibars, Sultan of Egypt in Antioch – 1268

The Fourth Crusade had aimed to attack Egypt as it had become the centre of Muslim power. By 1260, that power was in the hands of a vicious former army general named Baibars. In 1265 Baibars launched a full-scale **jihad** against the crusader states. Using his massive army and a range of cunning deceptions, he took one crusader city or castle after another. In 1268 his forces gathered outside the mighty walls of Antioch, which, in 1097, had only fallen to the crusaders after eight months of desperate siege. Baibars took it in a single day. His army slaughtered the inhabitants who had so foolishly refused to surrender.

Baibars died in 1277 before his victory over the Franks was complete. He was buried in Damascus close to the tomb of Saladin. In the years that followed, the Muslims pressed home their advantage. In 1291 they recaptured the last crusader city, the port of Acre. The age of the Crusades to the Holy Land was over.

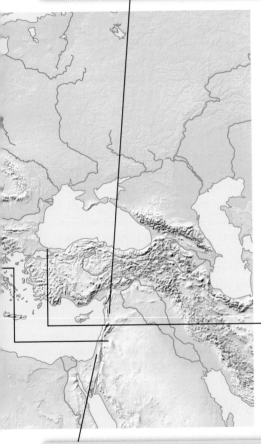

Story 5: Enrico Dandolo in Constantinople – 1204

In 1198 Pope Innocent III called a Fourth Crusade in a bid to put Jerusalem once and for all under Christian control. Its leaders planned to launch their attack on Muslim lands by sea. They worked with Enrico Dandolo, the Doge (leader) of Venice. This Italian sea power had grown rich by trading in the Mediterranean. Dandolo was blind and over 90 years of age when he agreed, not only to provide the ships to take a crusader army to attack Egypt, but also to join the Crusade himself.

The Crusade was a shameful disaster. Dandolo and the other leaders took their fleet to Constantinople, not Egypt, hoping that the Byzantine Christians of the city would support them. But the crusaders became involved in a brutal and treacherous Byzantine civil war, and ended up capturing Constantinople. The Crusade never reached Egypt. Instead, western Christians fought eastern Christians and a Flemish nobleman took over as the new Byzantine Emperor. Meanwhile, Dandolo and others looted the treasures of Constantinople and sent them home to Venice. The crusader states were left to look after themselves.

Story 4: Saladin in Jerusalem – 1189

When the first crusaders took Jerusalem in 1099, the Muslim world was too divided to resist the power of the Franks. That changed in the second half of the twelfth century with the emergence of a new leader in the Muslim **Near East**. His name was Saladin. In 1187 his army shattered the Franks at the Battle of Hattin to the north of Jerusalem. Within weeks he took Jerusalem itself. The city was back in Muslim hands for the first time in almost 90 years. In an attempt to regain Christian control of Jerusalem, a Third Crusade (1189–92) set out from Europe. In England this campaign is famous for the part played by King Richard I. He forced Saladin to stop his attacks on the crusader states, but Jerusalem remained under Muslim control.

What does this book try to do?

This book helps you to develop a deep understanding of the Crusades. We have structured it around enquiry questions covering the period from 1095 (the First Crusade) to 1204 (the Fourth Crusade). Each one focuses on fascinating people, places and events. Our book also includes 'insights' that allow you to explore particular aspects of the Crusades in more depth. These enquiries and 'insights' will help you to:

1 Enter the minds of people in the past

How were crusades justified? What motivated the crusaders? How did Christians and Muslims relate to each other during the time of the Crusades? These are big questions that the enquiries and 'insights' in this book will help you to answer. We should always remember that history is about real people living through particular moments in time. The people you will read about in this book faced tough situations and difficult decisions. The world they inhabited was very different from ours. It takes a huge effort of imagination to enter their minds; but that's what good historians do.

2 Make up your own mind

Historians love to debate and argue. In the 1980s they began to argue about the definition of 'the Crusades'. Some historians (*Traditionalists*) insisted that the only real crusades were those that tried to capture or defend the city of Jerusalem and they limited their studies to the period 1095–1291. Your A Level course is probably shaped by this interpretation. Others (*Pluralists*) argued that a crusade was any war proclaimed by the Pope, whether against Muslims, fellow Christians, people with **pagan** beliefs or simply political enemies. In their minds, the Crusades lasted into the eighteenth or nineteenth century. This book does not get deeply involved in that old debate but it does try to help you decide about other arguments between historians about the motivation of the crusaders, the reasons behind the outcomes of different Crusades, and the ways in which Muslims and Christians related to each other. By encouraging you to wrestle with these issues, this book helps you to strengthen your own mind and to develop the healthy habit of supporting your opinions with evidence.

3 Discover how historians work

Our understanding of the past doesn't stand still. Each generation of historians builds on the work of earlier historians, challenging but also deepening previous understanding. As you read this book you'll find examples of historians challenging old ideas and putting forward new interpretations. Sometimes this happens because historians ask new and interesting questions. Interpretations also change because historians read the written sources (chronicles, letters, legal documents, poems and songs) in different ways, or because they look beyond the texts and ask interesting questions about the material remains of the Crusades – castles, settlements, art, coins and other artefacts. In this book you'll discover some of the ways in which historians work, and why the Crusades continue to be such a fascinating area of historical research.

4 Explore Muslim perspectives

In studying the Crusades we need to try to understand the experiences and attitudes of men and women, rich and poor, east and west, Christian and Muslim. This last point really matters. A feature of recent historical study of the Crusades has been the attempt to find sources that reveal the mind-set of Muslims during this period. We have attempted to reflect this by exploring the Crusades from both Christian and Muslim perspectives. In enquiries that focus on particular Crusades you will consider Muslim as well as Christian strategies and experiences. In Enquiry 4, when you investigate life in the crusader states, you will use both Christian and Muslim sources. In Enquiry 6 you will focus entirely on changes in the Muslim world.

5 Appreciate complexity

This book inevitably focuses on conflict and warfare. You will read about terrible acts of violence and slaughter. Against this backdrop it would be easy to view the era as an age of 'total war' between Islam and the west, an era of embittered conflict, fuelled by ingrained hatred and cycles of reciprocal violence. But people and societies are multi-layered. As you study the Crusades you will encounter warfare and violence alongside deep religious **piety** and human loyalty. You will find groups and individuals sometimes bitterly and brutally divided and sometimes working together in remarkable displays of respect and interdependence. Recent research has shown that the Crusades were not only about Christian Holy War and Islamic jihad, they also involved trade and cultural exchange between Christians and Muslims. The extraordinary complexity of the Crusades is something that we have tried to emphasise in this book.

6 Understand why the Crusades still matter

We believe that there has never been a more important time to study the Crusades. Religious conflict is a fact of life in the twenty-first century just as it was in the medieval world. Indeed, religiously justified violence is on the increase across the globe. Almost every day the news carries images and stories of murders committed in the name of religion. Many people engaged in religious conflict use the language of Holy War and of crusading to provide a moral justification for violence. Sometimes they even make direct links between the Crusades and current conflicts. Almost always these links are based on false perceptions and prejudices rather than on historical reality and careful study. In the final pages of this book we try to show just how dangerous the false perceptions can be.

So is this the only book I need?

Definitely not! Never rely on just one book when studying history. Success at A level can only come by engaging with a range of texts that provide different levels of detail and, quite possibly, argue different points of view. Which other books should you read? Ideally you will find books that have not just been written for A level, but ones that take you deeper. There are several strong histories of the Crusades available at the time of writing. You will find some suggestions at www.schoolshistoryproject.org.uk/Publishing/BooksSHP/Enquiring/Crusades.

Jerusalem – the holy city in the Holy Land

In AD985, about 100 years before the Crusades began, a Muslim named al-Muqaddisi wrote affectionately about the city where he was born. It was set in dry, rocky hills, about 30 miles from the south-eastern corner of the Mediterranean Sea. He called the city al-Quds, meaning 'The Holy', but we know it as Jerusalem.

Al-Muqaddisi accepted that the city had its faults: the public baths were dirty, the produce on sale was expensive and he complained that 'all the year round, never are her streets empty of strangers'. But he praised the fine stone buildings, and the cleanliness of the markets that sold grapes, oranges, figs, bananas and almonds of excellent quality. Water was freely available all around the city and there were no brothels. He noted with pride how the call to prayer went out from minarets across the narrow streets and alleyways, and he admired the beauty of the Aqsa Mosque high on the Temple Mount. Above all he delighted in the **Dome of the Rock**, lovingly describing the scene at dawn when the sun's rays fell on the brass-covered roof of this great shrine at the high point of the city. It marked the place where, in Muslim belief, the Prophet Muhammad had been taken on a sacred **Night Journey** from Earth to heaven so that God could teach him the secrets of prayer.

Al-Muqaddisi boasted that he had not heard of any building from pre-Islamic times that could match the Dome of the Rock. The city's history stretched back thousands of years before Muslim Arabs had captured it in AD638. In those centuries it had become sacred to two other religious groups: the Christians and the Jews. Different Jewish temples had occupied the exact site where the Muslims later put their Dome of the Rock. The first was built around 950BC by King Solomon, son of the great King David. The land it occupied became known as Temple Mount. In the course of the next thousand years, that temple was twice destroyed and twice rebuilt. The third temple was built by King Herod in 19BC, with the agreement of the Romans who had conquered the region but allowed him to continue as king of the Jews.

In that same period under Roman rule, a Jewish carpenter named Jesus began preaching in Jerusalem and the surrounding area. His teachings deeply upset the Jewish leaders who asked the Romans to put him to death. Around AD33, Jesus was crucified on a hill to the west of the city walls. His body was entombed nearby but his followers were convinced that he rose from the dead, proving that he was the son of God. Their certainty created the new religion of Christianity. It survived and spread far and wide, despite the efforts of the Romans to crush it.

In AD70 the Romans also turned against the Jews who – like the Christians – now refused to submit to the Roman Emperor. The Romans pulled down Herod's temple and in AD130 the Emperor Hadrian went further and banned all Jews from Jerusalem. Most left the city though some later returned and there has always been a Jewish presence there over the centuries. Thousands of Jews travelled each year to pray at the mighty walls that support the Temple Mount.

Jerusalem lost importance over the next 200 years, but that changed in AD326. In that year the Roman Emperor Constantine, who had recently announced that Christians could now worship freely, sent his mother Helena to Jerusalem. She had become a Christian and longed to honour the place where Christ had died and had risen. She ordered the building of a glorious church on the exact site of the crucifixion and of the tomb. When the Muslims conquered the region in the seventh century, they did not destroy this Church of the Holy Sepulchre, accepting that Jesus had been a prophet, but not the Son of God. They allowed Christians and Jews to live in the city and to follow their own religions provided they paid a special tax each year.

The Muslims also allowed **pilgrimages** to continue. As the Church of the Holy Sepulchre was being built, Helena claimed that workers had found the cross on which Christ had died. This True Cross was placed within the church and many thousands of Christian pilgrims, from as far away as western Europe, flocked to Jerusalem each year just to pray before it. They mixed with Jews who came to pray at the walls of the Temple Mount and the Muslims who travelled from afar to see the Dome of the Rock. No wonder al-Muqaddisi complained that the streets of Jerusalem were always full of strangers. Muslims, Christians and Jews all felt that this city belonged to them.

This shows the area of Jerusalem from the time of Jesus to the early twentieth century.

Temple Mount, the site of the ancient temple of the Jews. The first temple was built by King Solomon around 950BC.

The Dome of the Rock, a holy Muslim shrine, built in AD692. The Aqsa mosque, built at about the same date, is marked to the right.

The Church of the Holy Sepulchre, originally built in AD330. Much of the building today dates from about AD1150.

2 Why did the First Crusade erupt in 1095?

Clermont has grown since the Middle Ages, It is now known as Clermont-Ferrand. You can just make out the dark, volcanic moutains in the distance.

This photograph shows the city of Clermont in central France. It occupies a dramatic setting on a high plain surrounded by a great ring of dormant volcanoes. The volcanoes seem very appropriate because it was from this ancient city, in 1095, that there erupted a movement of such dramatic power and energy that its repercussions still affect our world today. We call it the First Crusade.

On the face of it, the cause of this explosion of crusading force was a sermon delivered not far from the site where the thirteenth-century cathedral now stands. On 27 November 1095, a crowd of several hundred gathered in a field just outside the ancient city to hear the words of a special visitor, the leader of the Church in western Europe, Pope Urban II.

In his great speech the Pope was passing on an urgent plea for help that had been sent to him earlier that year. It came from the Emperor Alexios I who ruled the distant Byzantine Empire thousands of miles to the east. Urban's words were powerful: within weeks, his message had been carried all over western Europe. Observers at the time recognised that something completely new was happening. As the shock waves spread, somewhere between 50,000 and 100,000 men and women, rich and poor, headed east for the Holy Land confident that they were doing the Pope's will and God's will. They were going to fight Muslims to win control of what they believed to be the holiest place on God's Earth: the city of Jerusalem.

■ Enquiry Focus: Why did the First Crusade erupt in 1095?

Events as resounding as the First Crusade cannot simply appear from nowhere. No matter how moving Pope Urban II's sermon may have been, one man's words cannot on their own change history. We need to look deeper if we are to understand what caused the First Crusade. Just like the eruption of a volcano, events like this are usually created by deep and powerful forces that have been rumbling away and building over many years. It just needs some shifts and changes to take place for that energy to burst into life.

The events behind the First Crusade go back many centuries and cover a wide geographical area, from Arabia in the east to France in the west. It also involves three main groups. These are:

- the eastern (Greek) Christians of the Byzantine Empire
- the western (Latin) Christians of western Europe
- the Muslims.

As so often in history lots of other questions are hiding below the big enquiry question we have given you. We have structured the enquiry to help you tackle these stage by stage as the summary below shows:

	The stages of the enquiry	'Hidden' questions that you will be considering
1	Weakening empires: Trouble in the Near East, 330 to 1071	What was happening in the Near East that made the Byzantine Emperor Alexios ask for help from western Christians?
2	The plea for help: Alexios I, 1071 to 1095	
3	The crusaders' world: Western society, 476 to c.1040	What was it about life in the western world that made so many Christians answer the call to fight an unknown enemy thousands of miles from home?
4	The power of popes: Church reform, c.1040–95	
5	The call to action: Urban II and the Council of Clermont, 1095	Why did Pope Urban II help Alexios I and how did he achieve such a massive response from western Christians?

Whatever question they are tackling, historians always need to respond with strong, relevant ideas backed up with carefully selected supporting evidence. To help you in this enquiry we will be giving you three 'main points' at the start of each section. Your challenge is to identify and select really useful, short but precise 'support points' for each one. At the end of the enquiry you will use these main points and support points to answer a host of different questions, including the main enquiry question: 'Why did the First Crusade erupt in 1095?'

Weakening empires: Trouble in the Near East, 330 to 1071

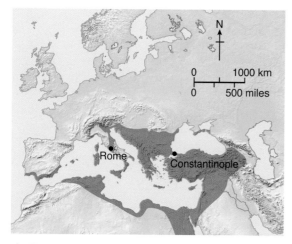

△ The Roman Empire c. AD600.

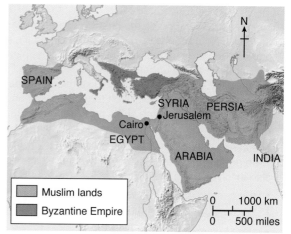

△ Muslim lands c. AD750.

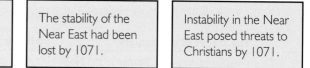

Muslim lands

Byzantine Empire

Here are the first three main points you will be using to explain why the First Crusade erupted in 1095. As you work your way through this section, make short, precise notes for each one, so that you can support the point that it makes.

Jerusalem never lost its importance for Christians.

The stability of the Near East had been lost by 1071.

Instability in the Near East posed threats to Christians by 1071.

The Byzantine Empire

To understand why the Crusade was proclaimed in the west in 1095, we first need to understand forces that had been at work for centuries in the east. These maps should help.

On the left you see the Roman Empire as it was in AD600. By that date the Romans had left Britain and most of western Europe but their empire had not disappeared completely. It lived on for many centuries in the east. Its capital city moved from Rome to Constantinople, the Greek-speaking city where Europe and Asia almost touched. It was in AD330 that the Roman Emperor, Constantine, moved the capital there and named it after himself. The old Greek name for the city was Byzantium so the Roman Empire in the east became known as the Byzantine Empire.

Constantine's other great change was to accept Christianity as the official religion of the entire Roman Empire. As you saw on pages 10 and 11, this meant that the city of Jerusalem, was officially recognised as a place of enormous significance. For over three centuries dating from AD326, when Constantine sent his mother there to supervise the building of the Church of the Holy Sepulchre, Jerusalem was ruled as a Christian city and grew to be a great centre of pilgrimage. After fighting a lengthy and exhausting war to expel an invading army from Persia in the first part of the seventh century, Jerusalem's place in the Christian Byzantine Empire seemed secure – but it was not.

The Muslim Empire

In AD610, in a cave in southern Arabia, the Prophet Muhammad believed God had revealed to him a new religion, now known as Islam. Before he died in 632, Muhammad saw this Muslim faith spread with extraordinary speed. Driven on by their belief in jihad, lightly armed but fiercely committed warriors carried the faith far beyond its birthplace.

In 637 the Muslims took **Palestine**. At the Battle of Yarmuk they simply wiped out the Byzantine Christian forces, which had been greatly weakened by their recent, long war with Persia. The following year the Muslim **Caliph**, Omar, accepted the surrender of Jerusalem in person. It is said that he respectfully rode through the main gates unarmed and dressed in the rough, white robes of a Muslim pilgrim. Omar found the Christians had been using the Temple Mount as a rubbish tip, but ordered that it be cleared so that he could pray on the holy site where Muslims would soon build the Aqsa Mosque and the Dome of the Rock.

In keeping with Muslim practice, the Christian and Jewish populations of Jerusalem were allowed to follow their own religion so long as they paid a special tax called the jizya. They also had to accept certain restrictions such as wearing distinctive clothes, not riding horses or trying to convert or marry Muslims. This relative tolerance allowed a fairly small number of Muslims to rule over a larger population of Christians and Jews. It also explains why, hundreds of years after it fell to Islam, Jerusalem still had a largely Christian culture, even though many inhabitants had probably become Muslims. Churches and holy sites still existed, customs were maintained and pilgrims still flooded in from all over the Christian world, even though the True Cross and other **relics** had been taken to Constantinople for safe keeping.

The Battle of Yarmuk had been such a devastating loss that, although they defended their lands in **Anatolia**, the once mighty Byzantines were too weak to launch any effective counter attacks against the Muslims. Instead, this Islamic empire spread even further and with extraordinary speed across north Africa. By AD750 Muslims ruled an empire that stretched from the Iberian peninsula (the lands we know today as Spain and Portugal) all the way to northern India (see the map on page 14).

Stability

Quite soon after 638, a border that was more or less stable was established between Muslim-held lands and the Byzantine Empire. This followed roughly the line we now recognise as the southern and eastern borders of modern Turkey. Over the following centuries there were occasional wars in that border region and, in the Mediterranean, the Muslims managed to take the island of Sicily and some parts of southern Italy from the Byzantines. But these wars were really more about land than religion. The zealous commitment to jihad, so obvious in the early years of Islam, seems to have waned.

As for the Byzantines themselves, they had no strong drive to interfere in **Syria** and Palestine. The churches there were not being persecuted and did not ask for outside help. The Greek Byzantine church had no Christian teaching equivalent to jihad that might have commanded them to make war against Islam, especially as the Muslims still allowed Christians from all over Europe to travel as pilgrims to Jerusalem. They did no harm and they brought trade to the city.

This coin was made in modern Turkey in 1971. It shows Alp Arslan, who led the Seljuk Turks to victory at Manzikert in 1071.

His moustache may look large here, but sources from the time say he would throw both ends back over his shoulders as he rode into battle!

Instability

In the second half of the tenth century the picture began to change. From their base in Baghdad, the ruling Muslim family, the **Abbasids**, were losing their hold on power. As they weakened, the Muslim world destabilised. This allowed Byzantine armies to regain a foothold in northern Syria by capturing the city of Antioch in 969. In that same year a rival Muslim group, the **Fatimids**, broke free from Abbasid control and took charge of Egypt and Palestine, including Jerusalem. Struggles between Fatimids and Abbasids in the Near East made pilgrimages much harder in the last years of the tenth century. Then, in 1009, a mentally deranged Fatimid ruler, Caliph Hakim, who had already persecuted many of his own Muslim people, suddenly ended the toleration of Christianity and ordered the complete destruction of the Church of the Holy Sepulchre. Pilgrimages stopped and in Europe anger towards Muslims grew, although no one felt strong enough or concerned enough to raise an army to take revenge. The Fatimid rulers who came after Hakim quickly did all they could to restore relations with Christians. They invited Byzantine architects to rebuild the Holy Sepulchre church and re-opened the city to Christian pilgrims. The crisis had passed.

Just as the pilgrimage numbers seemed to be fully restored by the middle of the eleventh century, another group emerged to take advantage of the continued weakening of Abbasid power. This was a fierce and ambitious people from central Asia: the Seljuk Turks. This tribe had converted to Islam in the late tenth century. In the 1040s they moved into the area we now call Iraq and by 1059 they had forced the Abbasid family to let them rule all their lands on their behalf. In practice this led to a time of lawlessness. In 1064 over 5000 Christian pilgrims from Germany and Flanders were brutally butchered in a single attack by Muslim tribesmen. This was not typical and many pilgrims continued to make their way to and from Jerusalem successfully, but safety could not be taken for granted.

Some Seljuks could not stop themselves from pressing for new land as well. In 1071, when they tried to move into the eastern Byzantine Empire, the Emperor tried to turn them back, but the Seljuks crushed the Byzantine army at the Battle of Manzikert. Breakaway Seljuk groups and other Turks from Asia began moving into unprotected Byzantine territory in Anatolia taking rich farmlands for themselves. Meanwhile the Seljuk leader, **Sultan** Alp Arslan, turned his armies south and took Syria, Palestine and Egypt, destabilising the region still further.

■ Check that the notes you have made support each of the main points shown on page 14.

How might each main point help to explain why the First Crusade erupted in 1095?

The plea for help: Alexios I, 1071 to 1095

> The Byzantine Empire was very weak by 1081.

> Alexios I's tactics for defending the Empire created closer links with western Christians.

> In 1095, Alexios I decided the time had come to drive the Seljuks from Anatolia.

> ■ Here are the main points for this section. Once again, as you work your way through this section, make short, precise notes for each one, so that you can support the point that it makes.

Threats on all sides

The Seljuks' victory at Manzikert shocked and shamed the population of Constantinople. For most of its history, the Byzantine Empire boasted one of the greatest armies in the world, but by 1050 it was in serious decline. In previous centuries, peasants who lived on the emperor's land had to serve in his army, but after AD1000 a series of emperors sold this land to rich families. Naturally the number of peasants who owed military service fell. The army was being weakened just when the Empire faced attack from three sides:

In the north, fierce pagan tribes crossed the river Danube in the 1050s. They forced the Byzantines to let them settle within the Empire. It seemed certain that they would push further before too long.

In the south, the Seljuks controlled so much of Anatolia by 1077 that they declared it to be their own and called it the **Sultanate of Rum** (their version of 'Rome'). In their minds they had conquered the old Roman Empire in Asia. In fact, many key cities of Anatolia, especially around the west coast, were still fairly securely held by local Byzantine rulers or by **Turks** who had done deals with Alexios I. Nonetheless, much valuable land had been lost to the Seljuks and the fairly stable border that had lasted for so many years between the Byzantine Christians and the Muslims had been shattered.

△ **Threats to the Byzantine Empire** c. 1070.

In the west, the Byzantine lands in Italy had been taken by a warlike people who first moved into the area around 1015. These were the Normans. They were from the same northern French families who conquered England in 1066. In 1071 the Norman leader, Robert Guiscard (nick-named Robert the Cunning), captured the last Byzantine possession in Italy, the southern city of Bari. By 1081, Robert was planning a full-scale invasion of the Byzantine lands in the **Balkans**.

17

The young emperor

In February 1081, fearing that the Empire would collapse if he did not intervene, a powerful general in the Byzantine army used bribery, deception and family ties at court to make himself the new Byzantine Emperor. On Easter Day 1081 a dark, powerfully built, twenty-four-year-old took the Byzantine imperial throne as Emperor Alexios I.

The situation that Alexios I inherited was perilous. Within a month of being crowned Emperor, he faced a massive Norman invasion of the Balkans. He had to reinforce what remained of the weakened army with **mercenaries** hired from far and wide. These included Vikings from Scandinavia, Franks from northern France and Anglo-Saxons from England, some of whom had recently fought against a different Norman invasion in 1066. Alexios even brought in Turks from Asia, including some who had recently helped to conquer Byzantine lands in Anatolia.

△ The Byzantine Emperor, Alexios I, being blessed by Christ, from a twelfth-century manuscript. Alexios, like Christ, is shown with a halo to suggest that he has been chosen and blessed by God.

He would use any warriors with a reputation for skill in battle and who were prepared to fight for a fee.

The young emperor also bought the support of the navy of Venice, a growing sea power in northern Italy. He granted the Venetians trading privileges in Constantinople in return for their help. They were delighted to win this advantage over their rivals. Venice had been gradually building trading links with the Byzantine Empire in the eleventh century. The Venetians did manage to destroy quite a few Norman ships carrying troops from Italy to the Byzantine lands in the Balkans. But, despite these losses, Robert Guiscard, ably assisted in battle by his ferocious wife and his ambitious son Bohemund of Taranto, won a victory over the Byzantine army in 1081.

In the end Alexios I saved his lands in the Balkans by paying the Pope's enemy, Henry IV, the German Emperor, to launch an attack on Rome. He knew that the Pope would call at least some of the Norman army back to Italy to defend him. This is exactly what happened in 1082. More through his cunning than military power, Alexios was safe, at least for a short time.

When Robert Guiscard's Norman armies attacked the Empire again in 1084, it was luck rather than money or planning that saved Alexios. After defeating the Venetians at sea, the Normans were all set to march on Constantinople, but an epidemic (probably typhoid) killed thousands of their soldiers, including Robert himself. The immediate threat from the Normans was over but Alexios had been greatly impressed by their ability to fight.

In that same year, 1084, Alexios once again spent enormous sums on mercenaries to launch a counter attack against the pagans who had occupied the northern Byzantine lands in the 1050s. By 1091 the tribes had been completely defeated. He could now turn his attention to the threat in the south – the Seljuk Turks.

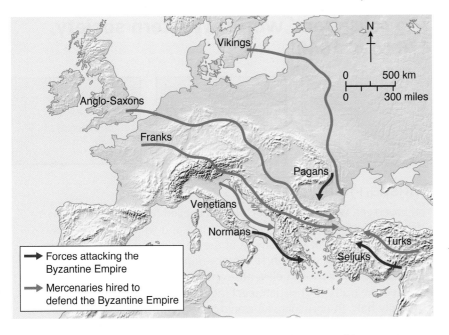

◁ Map showing how foreign forces were being drawn into the Byzantine Empire c. 1050–95.

While Alexios had been fighting in the north and the west of his Empire in the 1080s, Seljuk and other Turkish warlords extended their power in Anatolia. They even took important cities such as Antioch and Nicaea, which was barely 60 miles from Constantinople. For some years the Seljuk sultan, Malik Shah, the son of Alp Arslan, worked with Alexios to limit Seljuk expansion in Anatolia. The sultan wanted to stop rival warlords there from becoming too powerful. But in 1092 Malik Shah died just weeks after his chief adviser had been murdered. The loss of these two men created a power vacuum in Anatolia. Rival warlords rushed to take all the land they could. By 1094 many important coastal towns had fallen to Seljuk lords. The situation was serious, but Alexios could now take on the Seljuks as he had defeated the enemies who had been attacking his other borders.

Most historians argue that Alexios was in a position of relative strength by 1095: he had defeated the Normans and the pagan tribes and he had built up his finances by melting down treasure from churches and from the imperial palaces to make new coins. He had also raised taxes. Certainly his daughter Anna Komnena, who wrote a history of her father's life, records that Alexios was more than ready to take on the Seljuks. But some specialists on Byzantine affairs insist that the new coins and high taxes were crippling the economy and that Alexios was losing the confidence of his people. His nobles insisted that he must win back the wealthy lands of Anatolia. Either way, from confidence or desperation, he decided to gather an army that could push the Seljuks back and recapture the lands they had taken since 1071. Early in 1095 he decided to ask for help from the Christians of western Europe, whose knights were renowned for their fighting skill. He sent letters to various western lords urging them to send knights to fight alongside the Byzantine army. But his most significant act was to send ambassadors to the leader of the Latin Church, Pope Urban II.

■ Check that the notes you have made support each of the main points shown on page 17.

How might each main point help to explain why the First Crusade erupted in 1095?

The crusaders' world: Western society, 476 to *c.* 1040

Here are the main points for this section. Once again, as you work your way through this section, make short, precise notes for each one, so that you can support the point that it makes. This section is a little longer than the ones you have done so far.

The fear of hell and purgatory shaped the lives of western Christians.

Western lords and knights were famous for being powerful warriors.

The Church was closely involved in the violence of society.

Christian faith

You have seen why the Emperor Alexios I called for help from western Christians in 1095. Now you need to understand what made them so ready to respond. Not surprisingly, at the heart of the matter lies religion.

It is hard for our twenty-first-century minds to imagine the importance of faith to people's lives in eleventh-century Europe. Almost everyone accepted the truth of Christian teaching even if their own lives were not especially holy. In particular, all would believe in the existence of heaven and hell. To them, these were real, physical places, not just abstract ideas.

The hope of heaven and the fear of hell was communicated through images such as those carved over the doorway to the church at Conques in southern France around 1100 (see the photograph on page 21). High on the left, Christ sits in judgement over mankind at the end of time. To his right, the saved are being welcomed into heaven, but that is not shown here. Instead, this image shows those on his left-hand side – the damned. Four angels block any chance of these sinners reaching heaven. Below Christ's feet, facing each other, another angel and a demon weigh each soul to judge whether it should pass to heaven or hell. The cord between the angel's hand and the two balances in the scales have crumbled away, but you may be able to see the demon trying to tip the scales in his favour by pushing down with his finger! Behind and below this demon, all sorts of suffering is being inflicted in hell.

Penance and penitence

This hope of heaven and fear of hell explains the medieval doctrine of **penance** and acts of **penitence**. The Latin Church taught that Christ's death and resurrection opened the way to heaven but only if people confessed their sins to priests who would grant them forgiveness, in God's name. But, even after confession, a believer's soul still needed to be cleansed of sins committed on Earth. This meant that, after death, the soul would spend time in **purgatory** being purged.

The cleansing of the soul in purgatory involved a prolonged period of pain and suffering, but this could be limited if the person carried out 'acts of penitence'. These might involve saying prayers, giving alms (money) to the poor, avoiding food or sexual activity, or going on a penitential pilgrimage to a holy site. During the eleventh century more and more Christians travelled to, and were obsessed by, the holiest and most sacred site of all: the Church of the Holy Sepulchre in the city of Jerusalem.

Most holy sites also kept relics. These were believed to hold special powers that reflected a saint's close relationship with God. They ranged from shreds of the dead saint's clothing or fragments from the coffin to parts of the body (such as bones, hands or even heads) or glass phials filled with blood. From the tenth century, a trade grew up in relics and many were simply stolen to be taken from one holy place to another. People assumed that God would only allow the object to be removed if He approved of the new home for the relic.

A pilgrimage by a penitent sinner to pray before a relic at a holy site might produce a miracle such as healing, or so it was commonly believed. But the main purpose of pilgrimage was penitential: suffering a long, hard journey was worth the pain if it would allow a soul to pass more quickly to the greatest prize – a place in heaven for eternity. The more special the relic or site, and the more hardship the penitent endured, the more powerful it was in washing the soul. What every Latin Christian most prized was a full **indulgence**. This was a promise of complete forgiveness so that the person's soul could pass straight to the joys of heaven, needing no acts of penitence or cleansing in purgatory. This was rare and very special and usually reserved only for the rich and powerful. But – as we shall see a little later – that changed in 1095, when Pope Urban II made a remarkable announcement.

△ Part of the portal at Conques Abbey, France. It was built at almost exactly the same date as the First Crusade. Originally it was painted in bright colours to add to the effect of the terrors it showed.

■ How might belief about heaven, hell and purgatory help to cause the Crusade?

Christian violence

You may be puzzled by the heading above. But consider these two descriptions:

He was a deeply religious man. The fear of hell drove him to seek God's forgiveness: he built a great abbey; he collected relics; he went on long pilgrimages; he ended one pilgrimage by walking naked to the place in Jerusalem where he believed Jesus had risen from the dead. As he walked, he prayed for forgiveness while, as a sign of humility, he allowed his servant to beat his bare back with a stick.

He was a cruel and violent man. When he learned that his young wife had been unfaithful to him, he had her burned alive in her wedding dress. He murdered a rival and may also have murdered his own grand-nephews. He stole valuable property, even from churches. He fought many brutal battles to take the lands of his near neighbours, slaughtering enemy soldiers without mercy.

Surprisingly, both these descriptions are about the same man: Count Fulk Nerra of Anjou. Fulk was a French nobleman. He lived from 972 to 1040. This extreme example shows us that medieval people could be genuine believers and still live cruel, greedy and violent lives.

A broken and brutal society

The western world in the eleventh century was a strange mix of all-pervading religion and regular bloodthirsty violence. It had been that way for hundreds of years since the fall of the Roman Empire in western Europe, around 476. Political power was fragmented. There was a brief period of unity around 800 under the French King Charlemagne who declared himself the Emperor of western Europe, but soon after his death his empire broke up and power returned to the regions.

Kings might claim to rule a large area, but in effect each locality was in the hands of a lord (like Count Fulk) who ruled as he wished. Land meant power, bringing the labour and taxes from all who lived on it. Lords were regularly drawn into wars with their neighbours to take extra land or to settle disputes between rivals. This culture of violence disturbed the entire local society: peasants became foot-soldiers and farming and trade was disrupted. No one could hide from the effects.

Just below the nobility were knights, men who had enough wealth to supply their own horse, armour and weapons. Most inherited this wealth as land. The custom on the continent of Europe was that a father's lands would be shared among all his sons on his death. Over time, this divided land into smaller portions and increased both the number of knights and the likelihood of violent land disputes. By the eleventh century, knights often terrorised their own neighbourhoods in their attempts to increase their power. Even when they were enforcing the law, they imposed vicious, physical punishments rather than fines. It was brutal, but it all helped to make these men highly effective warriors.

You might imagine that the Church would be horrified at such a culture of violence. Some Christian leaders did speak out against it but, by the start of the eleventh century, the Church in western Europe was simply another part of this brutal society. Duke William of Normandy's conquest of England in 1066 is a well-known example of a powerful lord settling a dispute by violence. What is less well known is that his brother Odo fought alongside him at the Battle of Hastings – and Odo was a Bishop.

The warrior aristocracy and wealthy knights funded monasteries and churches, while bishops or abbots like Odo, often from the same powerful families as the lords, led knights into battle. Around AD1000, one French knight brutally butchered a man who had murdered his brother. He then gave the murderer's blood-soaked armour to the local monastery as a way of thanking God for his success. The monks accepted the gift.

A Just War

Later we shall see how the Church eventually tried to end the worst excesses of this violent way of life, but even then it never attempted to take a fully pacifist position. Centuries before, when the Roman emperors first made Christianity the official religion of the Empire, the Church had developed teachings to explain why it was acceptable for the state to build and use mighty armies in war. In the fifth century, one of the early Church's greatest thinkers, St Augustine, a north African bishop, set down the conditions under which Christians could wage war:

- The war must be proclaimed by a legitimate authority, such as a king or bishop. It could not be done on the whim of an individual.
- The war must be in a just cause, such as defending people against an enemy attack.
- The war must show 'right intention'. It should be restrained, using the minimum violence necessary to achieve its aims.

If it met all these conditions, this could be a **Just War** – but Augustine maintained that it was still sinful for any Christian to fight even in these circumstances. The warrior would still need to pay for his sins with acts of penitence or hope for an indulgence. From this cautious starting point, the Church and Christian leaders grew more ready to engage in war over the following centuries.

> Check that the notes you have made support each of the main points shown on page 20.
>
> How might each main point help to explain why the First Crusade erupted in 1095?

△ The Battle of Hastings in 1066, from the Bayeux Tapestry. Duke William (right) is lifting his face visor. His brother, Bishop Odo, is towards the left, holding a club.

The power of Popes – Church reform, c. 1040–95

■ Here are the main points for this section. Once again, as you work your way through this section, make short, precise notes for each one, so that you can support the point that it makes.

| The Church reform movement increased piety. | The Church reform movement developed the theology and use of Holy War. | Urban II wanted to take Church reform even further. |

The reform movement

It was around 1040 that leading clergymen first set about challenging violence in society and weakness in the Church in a systematic and sustained way. They wanted to **reform** and renew the Church. The reformers were ashamed of what had happened in past centuries. Not only was the Church caught up in the violence of society, many priests were sinful or corrupt: they kept wives or mistresses and engaged in simony, the buying of promotion from local lords who had gained an unhealthy control over the Church in their area. The reformers always spoke of regaining *Libertas* or liberty for the Church. They were determined to win back its freedom from any external power that might fail to provide for the people of God whether it be a local lord or a king.

The person most closely identified with the reform movement was Pope Gregory VII who led the Latin Church from 1073 to 1085. He believed God had called him to restore purity and justice amongst Christians. Gregory improved the education of the clergy and tightened discipline over their sexual behaviour and their leading of worship. He also promoted a wave of church building which over the next centuries ensured that western Europe was covered by a network of parish churches. Better priests and more churches gradually led to deeper piety amongst lay people. In the second half of the eleventh century there were regions where influential families were fully committed to the reform movement – and many crusaders were to come from these areas.

Pope Gregory took on anyone who challenged the power of the **papacy**. This included the German Emperor, Henry IV, who claimed that he alone had the power to appoint Popes and that other kings and lords should therefore control the appointment or investiture of new bishops and other Church leaders. In 1075 Gregory declared that this was wrong and that only the Pope could appoint Church leaders. This led to a prolonged war between the papacy and the German Emperor. This is often called the Investiture Contest. This reached a low point in 1080, when Henry appointed a separate Pope and attacked Rome with his armies.

If it had not been for the Investiture Contest, some believe that there may have been some sort of crusade as early as the mid 1070s. When Gregory VII learned of the Seljuk movement into Byzantine lands at that time he announced that he would lead an army of Christian volunteers from Europe to drive them back. His plan had to be abandoned, though, as his struggle against the German Emperor meant he was too weak to see it through.

■ How would a war against the Seljuks fit the principle of *Libertas* mentioned earlier on this page?

From Just War to Holy War

Pope Gregory faced a strange paradox: if the reform movement was to survive and restore order to western society, it needed armed support from kings and lords – the very people he was hoping to restrain from inflicting violence on each other. The Church was now not just allowing wars, it was directing them, as in its struggle with the German Emperor and in Gregory's vain attempt to raise an army against the Seljuks. Some priests argued that the Church should fight violence with prayer, not with more violence. Gregory VII and Urban II needed to answer this criticism. For this reason, they actively supported a remarkable woman, Matilda, Countess of Tuscany. Not only did she use her own armies to defend the papacy against attack from the German Emperor, she also gathered a cluster of great scholars such as Bishop Anselm of Lucca, who built on the understanding of Just War that St Augustine had developed over 500 years before. The scholars found Bible verses and arguments to say that it was not only acceptable for people to fight against the enemies of the Church, it was their Christian duty to do so. But they still agreed with Augustine that it was a sin to kill another man in war, even a holy one.

The Church reform movement also wanted to end the general lawlessness across western society. As long ago as 989 a movement that became known as the 'Peace and Truce of God' had attempted to restrain the widespread violence against vulnerable members of society in France. Lords and knights were called upon to swear that they would end their violent ways. In some cases this movement even tried to ban violence on specific days of the week, but with little success. Gregory VII and his predecessor tried instead to exploit the warlike culture of western lords by encouraging them to take up arms against the enemies of the Church. Some are shown in this map:

> Pope Gregory VII's favourite Bible verse was from the Old Testament book of Jeremiah, Chapter 48, verse 10. It reads 'Cursed is he who keeps back his sword from bloodshed'. He was sure that God wanted Christians to fight to achieve God's will.

1 In 1066 the Pope blessed the armies of Duke William of Normandy before they invaded England, as he believed William's enemy King Harold had broken a holy vow.

2 In 1073 Gregory VII encouraged a violent French lord to try to re-conquer Spain from the Muslims.

3 In 1074 (in a sign of things to come) Gregory VII offered to lead an army against the Muslim Seljuk Turks who had invaded the lands of the Byzantine Empire. The plan came to nothing as Gregory was still struggling against the German Emperor.

5 In 1081 Gregory VII offered spiritual rewards to armies such as those of Matilda of Tuscany who fought for him against the German Emperor.

4 In 1076 Gregory VII promised that the sins of another group of Normans would be forgiven for fighting to take Sicily from the Muslims who ruled the island.

△ This statue of Pope Urban II stands near his birthplace at Châtillon in northern France. It was put up in 1887 almost exactly 800 years after he became Pope. It shows him sending the crusaders east.

Urban II strengthens the papacy

Gregory VII was still fighting against the armies of the German Emperor, Henry IV, when he died in 1085. Another Pope ruled for just three years until 1088 when a former adviser and close friend of Gregory's took over as the head of the Latin Church. This was Pope Urban II.

Urban came from a noble family in northern France. He had seen at close hand the world of lords and knights. He had worked at the Abbey of Cluny, one of great reforming monasteries, where he had become more and more committed to restoring order to the Church and holiness to the lives of its people. As Pope he was convinced that he must find ways to help their souls to heaven. He was also eager to try to bring greater unity to the Church. He was well aware that since 1054 there had been significant divisions and quarrels between the Latin Church in the west and the **Greek Church** in the Byzantine Empire to the east. This is sometimes called the Great Schism. Despite the fact that the Byzantine Emperor, Alexios I, had recently paid the German Emperor to attack the Pope's lands in Italy, Urban II sent messages of goodwill to Alexios. Together they eased the tensions between east and west, and weakened the German Emperor.

Meanwhile the papacy's war with the German Emperor continued. For several years Urban was exiled from Rome by the presence of German armies there. But he used his close knowledge of the noble classes and of Church leaders to build up a power base, particularly in France. Most importantly he continued the policy of Gregory VII and offered spiritual rewards to the Normans of southern Italy if they would drive the German Emperor's armies away from Rome. The plan worked and by 1094 he could claim to have the upper hand in the Investiture Contest.

In 1089 Urban once again tried to turn the warlike qualities of westerners to the advantage of the Church. He offered spiritual rewards to Christian knights if they would rebuild a city on the borders between Christian and Muslim lands in Spain. He assured them that this military work would count as much as a pilgrimage to Jerusalem as a penance for past sins. The Church and the military aristocracy of Europe were becoming regular partners in Just War. But none of these campaigns involved the mass involvement of Christian people. The opportunity for war on a far grander scale was to come in March 1095 when Pope Urban II received ambassadors from Alexios I at a Church council at Piacenza in Italy: with them they brought the Emperor's plea for help against the Seljuk Turks.

■ Check that the notes you have made support each of the main points shown on page 24.

How might each main point help to explain why the First Crusade erupted in 1095?

The call to action: Urban II and the Council of Clermont, 1095

Alexios I knew how to win western support.	Urban II had several reasons for offering support to Alexios I.	Urban II knew exactly how best to win mass support for the Crusade.

■ Here are the main points for this section. Once again, as you work your way through this section, make short, precise notes for each one, so that you can support the point that it makes.

The Emperor's plea and the Pope's plans

Through his ambassadors at Piacenza, Alexios I tried to make the most of the improved relations he had recently established with the Pope. He implored Urban II and all faithful Latin Christians to send armed men to defend 'the holy Church' by driving back 'the pagans' (meaning the Seljuks). According to Alexios, they were not only at the walls of Constantinople, but had been persecuting Christians who lived under Muslim control all over the Near East especially in Jerusalem, which made pilgrimages dangerous. He was almost certainly exaggerating all these claims in order to win western support. There is some evidence that Christians in the Near East did suffer after the Seljuks arrived but it was probably not as bad as Alexios claimed.

It is hard to know from the very few sources that remain exactly what Alexios really wanted by way of help. It is likely that he simply hoped for a large force of trained, armed soldiers to join him in driving the Seljuks out of Anatolia. It is just possible that he even wanted to reclaim Jerusalem for the Byzantine Empire for the first time since AD638, or he may have given that impression just to win recruits to his cause, knowing how precious Jerusalem was in the eyes of western Christians.

Whatever Alexios I intended, Pope Urban II certainly took the message seriously. Here was his chance to inspire the unruly lords and knights of western Europe to turn their weapons not on each other, but on the enemies of the Church. If he could achieve this, it would help pacify western society. Fighting against the Seljuks would also fit the Church reform movement's belief in *Libertas*, by freeing Christians from the rule of unbelievers. But there were political benefits too. If he could win the willing support of lords and knights for a Holy War in the east, he believed it might finally establish the papacy's superiority over the German Emperor.

The propaganda and the promise

On hearing this plea at Piacenza, Urban urged many to swear an oath that they would go to help Alexios and he started planning exactly how he would spread the message across the western Church. Over the next few months he prepared for another grand Church council to be held at Clermont in France in 1095. (This was the one that you read about at the start of this enquiry.) But well before he gave his sermon at Clermont, Urban had made every effort to ensure that his call to free Jerusalem would reach a wide audience among the people most likely to respond.

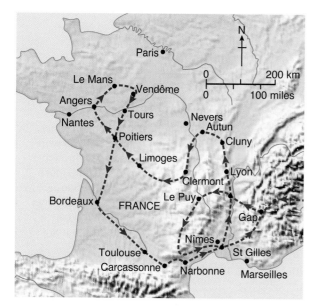

△ **Preaching tour of Pope Urban II 1095–96.**

To help you understand how carefully Pope Urban II prepared the ground and how effectively he spread his message, we have prepared an 'Insight' section on pages 30 and 31.

Look at the notes you have made on each of the main points shown on page 27.

How do they help to explain why the First Crusade erupted in 1095?

Before and after he gave his famous sermon at Clermont in November 1095, Urban travelled widely through France, preparing and following up his message. Urban's childhood as the son of a French nobleman helped him appeal to the powerful lords and bishops and the plentiful, aggressive knights of France. He also knew how to use the network of churches, abbeys and families closely committed to reform.

Quite apart from his carefully planned programme and his knowledge of his audience, it was what Urban actually said that created such a powerful response. His words went further than any previous Pope in promising spiritual rewards for those who fought for the Church. Although the only surviving accounts of his sermon were written after the capture of Jerusalem and must have been affected by hindsight and the joy of victory, letters and notes written by Urban in 1095 and 1096 make clear his central message. He brought several familiar Christian ideas together in a new context.

1   The idea of a long but spiritually rewarding pilgrimage.

2   The idea that war could be a Christian duty and an act of love for fellow Christians whose liberty had been taken away (in this case by Muslims, seen as unbelievers).

3   The idea of an indulgence that would remove the sinner's need for acts of penitence and ensure a swift passage of his soul to heaven.

It was the unprecedented union of these three ideas that was so powerful. For the first time, and on a grand scale, all Christians, rich and poor, were being promised by God's own representative on Earth, the Pope, that fighting in a war against the enemies of the Church would bring what so many deeply wanted: a full indulgence. It was effectively guaranteeing them the highest of prizes: a direct path to heaven and eternal salvation from the moment of death.

The message was carried quickly and powerfully across Europe, helped by the improved network of parish churches and by the religious enthusiasm that had been growing with the work of the reform movement. A sure sign of the effectiveness of the Pope's promise of indulgence was that Godfrey of Bouillon, who for years had served the German Emperor in wars against the papacy, switched sides. Within a few months he, along with many thousands more, had sewn a simple crusader cross onto his tunic and was part of a massive pilgrim army making its way to the Holy Land.

The First Crusade had erupted into life.

■ Concluding your enquiry

By now you should have notes to support each of the main points shown below. Many people find it helpful to thin notes down to the essentials by making notes on their notes. You could do this by copying each of these main points onto one side of a card and adding your bulleted support points on the reverse.

Of course these main points and their support points, do not, as they stand, answer the question about why the First Crusade erupted in 1095. You need to work with them and try to develop an argument. To sharpen your thinking and develop your ideas you could …

- Organise them by **IMPORTANCE**: This is quite a good way to start. Place the most important point at the top and the least at the bottom, but as you do so you will probably find they are often closely connected: one would not be important without another.

- Organise them by **TIME**: Separate long-term factors that created the conditions for the Crusade from the short-term factors that let it burst into life. Which would you call 'preconditions' rather than 'causes' and why?

- **BALANCE** one factor against others: Examiners like to set you this challenge where you have to take one possible factor and 'weigh up' how significant it was in causing the First Crusade. In your answer you would need to show you understand how that factor did play a part, but then move on to consider other factors which were either more or less significant than the one you were given. Examples might be:
  - the role of Urban II
  - the role of Alexios I
  - the Seljuk conquests
  - the weakness of the Byzantine Empire
  - the Church reform movement.

Jerusalem never lost its importance for Christians.	The stability of the Near East had been lost by 1071.	Instability in the Near East posed threats to Christians by 1071.
The Byzantine Empire was very weak by 1081.	Alexios I's tactics for defending the Empire created closer links with western Christians.	In 1095, Alexios I decided the time had come to drive the Seljuks from Anatolia.
The fear of hell and purgatory shaped the lives of western Christians.	Western lords and knights were famous for being powerful warriors.	The Church was closely involved in the violence of society.
The Church reform movement increased piety.	The Church reform movement developed the theology and use of Holy War.	Urban II wanted to take Church reform even further.
Alexios I knew how to win western support.	Urban II had several reasons for offering support to Alexios I.	Urban II knew exactly how best to win mass support for the Crusade.

Pope Urban II's sermon at Clermont

We have no exact record of Pope Urban II's famous sermon at Clermont. The only surviving accounts were written years later, after the capture of Jerusalem and were probably influenced by hindsight and the joy of victory. Official letters and notes written by Urban in 1095 and 1096 confirm that the central message in those accounts is probably accurate, although each sermon probably has exaggerations and emphasises certain points according to the author's own background and the audience he is writing for. Of course, even if the accounts did capture what Urban actually said, we cannot know whether the Pope had exaggerated or amended the pleas for help that had been sent to him by Alexios I.

You can see extracts from two sermon summaries and two official papal letters on these pages. They tell all sorts of things such as the motives that Urban appealed to, his view of Muslims and the sort of people he wanted to become crusaders.

Fulcher of Chartres gives his version of Pope Urban's sermon

Fulcher wrote this account around 1106. He was a priest who seems to have been at Clermont when the sermon was preached and who went on the First Crusade. Historians regard Fulcher's account of the First Crusade as one of the most straightforward, although he used his book to encourage Christians in Europe to become crusaders and to defend the newly conquered lands around Jerusalem.

… Your brethren in the east are in urgent need of your help … For, as most of you have heard, the Turks and Arabs have attacked them and have conquered Romania [the Byzantine Empire] as far west as the shore of the Mediterranean … . … and have killed and captured many Christians, and have destroyed the churches … If you permit them to continue … the faithful of God will be much more widely attacked by them. On this account I, or rather the Lord, beseech you to publish this everywhere and to persuade all people of whatever rank, foot-soldiers and knights, poor and rich, to carry aid promptly to those Christians and to destroy that vile race from the lands of our friends … Moreover, Christ commands it. All who die by the way, whether by land or by sea, or in battle against the pagans [Fulcher means the Muslims], shall have immediate remission of sins. This I grant through the power of God with which I am invested. O what a disgrace if such a despised and base race, which worships demons, should conquer a people which has the faith of omnipotent God and is made glorious with the name of Christ! … Let those who have been accustomed unjustly to wage private warfare against the faithful now go against the infidels!

Pope Urban's letter to Flanders, December 1095

To all the faithful, both princes and subjects in Flanders … We believe you have long since learned from many accounts that a barbaric fury has deplorably afflicted and laid waste the churches of God in the regions of the **Orient**. Worse still, it has seized the Holy City of Christ. Grieving with pious concern at this calamity we visited the regions of Gaul (France) and urged the lords and subjects of that land to free the churches of the east. We solemnly enjoined such an undertaking upon them for the remission of all their sins. We have appointed Adhemar, Bishop of Puy, leader of this expedition in our stead so that those of you who may wish to undertake this journey should comply with his commands.

Robert, the monk of Rheims gives his version of Pope Urban's sermon

Robert was a monk who did not take part in the First Crusade, but he claims to have been at Clermont when Pope Urban II preached in 1095. Robert's account was probably written by 1107. He uses earlier accounts by returning knights as his framework for describing the Crusade, but was instructed by his abbot to add literary style. He also seems to have been very aware of his French audience.

'Oh race of Franks … chosen and beloved by God … we wish you to know … what peril is threatening you and all the faithful. From Jerusalem and Constantinople a horrible tale has gone forth … A race from the kingdom of the Persians, an accursed race, a race wholly alienated from God… has violently invaded the lands of those Christians and has depopulated them by sword, pillage and fire. They destroy altars … torture people … rape the women. The kingdom of the Greeks is now dismembered by them … To whom therefore does the task of avenging these wrongs and recovering this territory fall, if not upon you? You, upon whom above all other nations God has conferred remarkable glory in arms, great courage and bodily energy. This land you inhabit … provides scarcely enough food for its cultivators, hence you murder and devour one another … Let therefore hatred depart from you, let your quarrels end … Take the road to the Holy Sepulchre, wrest that land from the wicked race and subject it to yourselves.'

When Pope Urban had said these things … all who were present cried out 'God wills it! God wills it!'

Pope Urban's letter to the churches in Bologna, September 1096

Whoever for devotion alone, not to gain honour or money, goes to Jerusalem to liberate the Church of God, can substitute this journey for all penance.

Pope Urban seems to have used what we would now call 'modern marketing strategies' to ensure the success of his call to crusade. Look again at page 28 and at these sources. You should be able to find examples of the following.

- A planned programme of activities across a wide area.
- A celebrity with a voice of authority.
- Theatrical or dramatic events to grab attention.
- Exploiting local links.
- Appealing to powerful human emotions, such as fear, guilt, duty, happiness.
- Exaggeration for effect.
- Strong emblems or icons to identify the new product.
- Catch phrases.
- Exploiting existing, popular attractions and values.
- Strong follow-up to initial launches.
- Special offers, never used before.
- Well-known figures who quickly endorse the product.
- Starting from places where your ideas or products are already popular.
- If possible, go 'viral'.

Curiously the one marketing technique that Urban missed was a strong brand name: the word Crusades was only used from about the thirteenth century.

3 Should we be surprised by the success of the First Crusade?

On 8 July 1099, Muslim soldiers looked out from the high stone walls that defended the ancient city of Jerusalem and laughed with derision. Below them in the dust, a bedraggled army of about 14,000 Christians walked barefoot around the city, singing and praying, led by their priests who carried a strange assortment of holy relics. The Muslims taunted the crusaders and fired arrows down on them without mercy whenever they passed within range. Over the previous four weeks, the crusaders had beaten against the massive walls of the city but the Muslims repelled their attacks with ease. How secure they must have felt behind their defences.

But just one week later the city fell. The Christians stormed over the walls and through the gates. Thousands of Muslims were put to the sword. The lords, knights, servants and pilgrims who had responded to the Pope's call in 1095 had struggled for almost four years to reach the holy city. Now, in just four weeks, their greatly reduced force had overcome the city's massive defences. For the first time since AD638, Jerusalem was in Christian hands.

△ The capture of Jerusalem in 1099 from a fourteenth-century French biography of Godfrey of Bouillon. Godfrey is shown wearing a crown. The image includes a mysterious knight who appeared on the Mount of Olives to direct the attack by waving his shield.

■ **Enquiry Focus:** Should we be surprised by the success of the First Crusade?

To the crusaders, the capture of Jerusalem was a miracle: they were sure that God had brought them through their various troubles and had delivered the holy city into their hands. But, as historians, should we be surprised that Jerusalem fell to the Christian army in 1099? Was it a victory against the odds? Or was it, in fact, always likely to happen?

This enquiry tells the story of the First Crusade. As you work your way through the narrative you should consider these three factors that may have helped or hindered the Christian attempt to take Jerusalem:

• **Motivation**: A successful army must be highly motivated. Was this true of the crusaders? If so, what did motivate them? Would it matter if different crusaders had different motives? Did their motivation change?

• **Leadership and tactics**: Successful armies need effective leaders who make wise plans, executing or adapting the plans as necessary. Was this the case with the crusaders who took Jerusalem?

• **Muslim opposition**: If the crusaders' opponents were strong and united, and if they exploited the advantage of fighting on home soil this would make a Christian victory truly surprising. But was this the case? Who were the Muslim leaders and how strong was their resistance?

For each of the five sections in this enquiry, capture your ideas and evidence in a table based on the one below. At the end of the enquiry, your five tables will help you weigh up whether we should be surprised by the 'miraculous' victory. To put it simply, if the evidence shows that the crusaders lacked motivation, were badly led and faced powerful opposition, we certainly should be surprised that they won!

How MOTIVATION helped the crusaders	How LEADERSHIP/TACTICS helped the crusaders	How weaknesses in the Muslim OPPOSITION helped the crusaders
How MOTIVATION hindered or failed the crusaders	How LEADERSHIP/TACTICS hindered the crusaders	How strengths in the Muslim OPPOSITION hindered the crusaders

We will tell the story of the First Crusade in five sections:

1 **The People's Crusade** – how the first wave of crusaders was utterly defeated. (November 1095 to October 1096)

2 **Preparations and Princes** – how the main wave gathered under its leaders and reached Constantinople. (November 1095 to December 1096)

3 **From Constantinople to Antioch** – how the Christians entered Muslim lands and reached the great city of Antioch. (May 1097 to October 1097)

4 **The siege of Antioch** – when the character of the First Crusade was defined. (October 1097 to July 1098)

5 **Antioch to Jerusalem** – how the Christians finally reached their goal and captured the holy city. (August 1098 to August 1099)

The People's Crusade (November 1095 to October 1096)

■ Remember to make notes using your first table based on the one on page 33. Use the heading 'The People's Crusade'.

The first wave of crusaders to leave Europe numbered 30,000. The leader, Peter the Hermit, was a preacher who travelled through northern France and Germany in the winter of 1095–96 delivering rousing sermons and urging people to take the cross. The force he gathered was poorly armed but deeply convinced of God's protection.

Peter's contingent set off in April 1096, four months before the departure date set by the Pope, who had no control over these events. Other groups, inspired by Peter, left at the same time from eastern France and southern Germany. In May and June some of these crusaders slaughtered thousands of Jews living in northern France and the Rhineland. The murderers saw little difference between Muslims in the Holy Land and Jews in Europe whose distant ancestors they blamed for the crucifixion of Christ. They were also keen to take the money of wealthy Jews who acted as money-lenders.

The journey east was long and difficult. The crusaders had no supplies. Thousands were killed by the armies of the King of Hungary as they raided his lands for food. When the rest reached Constantinople in August, the Emperor Alexios I was dismayed by their lack of military skill or discipline. He had them transported across to Asia and ordered them to wait for the Pope's main armies at a camp at Kibotos.

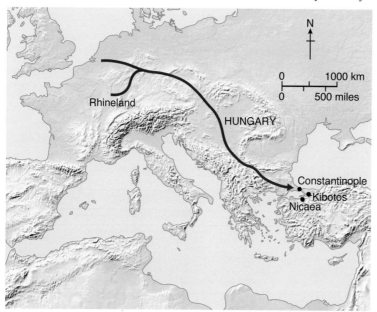

△ The People's Crusade 1095–96.

Their enemy, the Seljuk Turks, watched as these westerners (or 'Franj' as they called them) spilled into Asia. They had seen Franj before and admired their fierce warfare, but this was different: spies in the crusaders' camp were amazed to find thousands of poor men, women and children who could not possibly be part of an effective army.

In early September, some bored crusaders seeking glory, ignored the Emperor's instructions and left their camp intending to capture the Seljuk city of Nicaea. They believed God would protect them but they were quickly crushed by a powerful Turkish army led by Sultan Kilij Arslan. The only survivors were those who agreed to become Muslims and to work as slaves.

On 21 October 1096, the Seljuks attacked the Christian camp. Turkish archers, horsemen and foot-soldiers cut down the remaining Christian knights and soldiers and massacred almost every man, woman and child. The People's Crusade had been totally crushed. There had been no miracles and no victory. Only time would tell whether the next wave of crusaders would fare any better.

■ In the light of the experiences of the People's Crusade, suggest what the next wave of crusaders would need to do differently if they hoped to succeed.

Summarise your thoughts beneath the table you have made for this section.

Preparations and Princes (November 1095 to December 1096)

The evidence from charters

The next wave of crusaders was led by senior noblemen and it is often called 'The Princes' Crusade'. Recruitment was stongest in areas that had supported Pope Gregory VII's reform movement, from families with a tradition of pilgrimage to the Holy Land and from areas of France that Pope Urban II had visited in person.

The best evidence about who went on crusade is found in charters. These record arrangements made by knights and lords as they mortgaged or sold their lands to buy armour, weapons, horses and other equipment for themselves and the soldiers they gathered around them. For many years, historians believed crusaders were often younger sons who would not inherit the family lands and who hoped to win land and wealth in the east. According to this view, any supposedly spiritual motives were simply covering a selfish search for riches. Over the past 40 years, historians have reversed this view, largely on evidence from the charters. These reveal that crusading was a very expensive and risky business and that many first-born sons took part. A family might take on huge debts to fund even one knight and his servants to travel to Jerusalem and back. A crusader was more likely to lose wealth than gain it.

△ A thirteenth-century crusader charter drawn up in England.

> ■ Remember to make notes using your first table like the one on page 33. Use the heading 'Preparations and Princes'.
>
> In this section, concentrate on motivation and leadership.

Although charters certainly help us to know who went crusading, they may be less helpful in telling us why they went. They often state that the crusader wanted to free Jerusalem and win forgiveness for his sins, but it was usually the Church that took a would-be crusader's land and exchanged it for cash, so most charters were written by clergy. These priests might choose to record the Church's official view, masking any worldly motives such as a search for adventure, wealth, status and glory.

The charters tell us nothing directly about the thousands of people from the lower orders who took part. We have almost no direct evidence about their lives or motives. Most historians now accept that, in the complex mix of motives for crusading, deep-seated religious commitment rather than greed was the most common reason for taking the cross, but there may have been material reasons as well, given the hardships of life at the time. Several years of drought and poor harvests in the 1090s led to a widespread outbreak of a deadly disease called ergotism, caused by eating bread made from fungus-infected cereal. Against this background, the prospect of an adventure in the east that promised personal salvation and a chance of riches, must have seemed to be a risk worth taking.

> The question of what motivated crusaders is discussed in some detail on pages 130 and 131.

The Princes

■ What motives for crusading can you find in this group of princes?

Do you think it would matter to the success of the Crusade if the leaders had different reasons for taking part?

Whatever their reasons, in the spring and summer of 1096 many thousands across Europe took their crusader vows and joined the forces of one or other of the various princes, according to their social ties and local loyalties.

The summary below tells you about the senior nobles or princes from Europe who jointly led the First Crusade. Even amongst this small group we can detect a complex range of motives.

Count Hugh of Vermandois was the brother of 'Philip the Fat' (King Philip I of France). The King had recently been in a dispute with Pope Urban II after committing adultery. Count Hugh agreed to go on the Crusade to show the King's loyalty to the Pope.

Count Robert II of Flanders had close connections with Constantinople. His father, Robert I, had been a pilgrim to Jerusalem in 1089 and had formed a friendship with Emperor Alexios I at Constantinople. The following year Robert I sent 500 knights to fight for Alexios. When his father died in 1093, Robert II felt a duty to help eastern Christians and Alexios – and he knew how richly the Emperor rewarded those who helped him.

Duke Robert of Normandy was the son of William the Conqueror and brother of William II of England. Robert was constantly in dispute with his brother. William II was keen to see Robert leave Europe. He raised a special tax in England and provided Robert with the funds to join the Crusade.

Duke Godfrey of Bouillon owned lands in the German Empire and for years he fought for the German Emperor against the papacy. But Godfrey was a devout Christian as well as a highly effective warrior so he changed sides to serve the Pope and God by fighting to free Jerusalem from Muslim control. He took a group of monks with him on crusade as his religious advisers and supporters.

Count Stephen of Blois was the son-in-law of William the Conqueror but he was not a very good soldier. He was highly educated and wrote poetry. He was devoted to his very religious wife, Adela, and may have joined the Crusade to please her. A charter records his prayer that God should return him safely to his wife.

Count Raymond of Toulouse was the oldest, richest and most experienced of these senior lords. He was a close friend and supporter of Pope Urban II. At Clermont he was the first prince to agree to join the Crusade, and minor nobles within his territory soon followed. Raymond was a deeply religious man but proud and stubborn. He wanted to die in the Holy Land and sold all his lands to take an enormous group with him on crusade. This included his wife and infant son.

Bishop Adhemar of Le Puy was a close friend and keen supporter of Pope Urban II. He was both a devout Christian and an excellent soldier. The Pope made Adhemar his representative on the Crusade and asked him to chair the council of all these princes that jointly decided on strategy.

Prince Bohemund of Taranto was the son of Robert the Cunning, the Norman lord who ruled southern Italy and who had invaded the Byzantine Empire in the 1080s. Bohemund was a very fine soldier and had fought alongside his father against Alexios I at that time. He had expected to gain land in the Balkans but their invasion failed. He had not inherited his father's lands in Italy and was not very wealthy: he remained eager to gain land elsewhere.

The forces gather

The princes set off between August and October 1096. If size alone were the deciding factor, their combined armies had every chance of success. It is impossible to know the exact figures, but the total force, excluding non-combatants, probably numbered about 50,000 although some historians put the figure nearer to 100,000. This must have been the largest army Europe had seen since the height of the Roman Empire.

The diagram below shows a very tentative summary of the numbers and social status of each part of the fighting force.

At the head were the eight **princes**.

Below them were about 200 **lords** each wealthy enough to own several castles.

Next came about 6000 **knights** who fought on horseback. Some were almost lords, while others were in danger of slipping back into the group below.

The next group was made up of about 22,000 **well-equipped foot-soldiers** who could provide their own weapons.

Then came another mass of about 22,000 **poorer foot-soldiers** who were provided with basic weapons by the lords.

Along with these armed men went many thousands of non-combatants. These included wives and children, washerwomen, servants, grooms, and elderly pilgrims as well as the infirm, prostitutes and criminals. The entire force, including these, may have reached 100,000. Urban II had never expected so many to respond to his call. Crusaders from different regions in different nations spoke twenty different languages and used seven different currencies once the armies joined up. Its size and diversity meant that the army was always likely to be disorganised if not chaotic. But the fact that so many were willing to travel so far, risking death in a distant land for a common cause, did at least suggest an impressive commitment.

Pope Urban expected the princes to gather their forces at Constantinople where they would join the Byzantine army under the command of the Emperor Alexios I. The Emperor had arranged for supplies to be provided to the westerners as they crossed his lands in the Balkans. This was to prevent the wild foraging that had marked the progress of the People's Crusade earlier that year. He also sent Byzantine generals to ensure safe passage for the crusaders and to stop them looting towns or even taking territory along the way. But even as the first contingents arrived at Constantinople in October 1096 Alexios was by no means certain that his western allies could be trusted.

> ■ Check that you have used pages 35 to 37 to add more notes about motivation and leadership to your table.
>
> From all the notes you have made so far, are you surprised that this Princes' Crusade succeeded in taking Jerusalem?

37

From Constantinople to Antioch (May 1097 to October 1097)

The welcome at Constantinople

Remember to make notes using another table based on the one on page 33. This time, use the heading 'From Constantinople to Antioch'.

The Emperor Alexios I needed the loyal support of the Franks who were flooding into his capital city. He believed they had come mainly to win riches, so he met each of the princes in person on their arrival in Constantinople and thanked them for their help with gifts of gold and jewels. Bohemund of Taranto – who had fought bitterly against Alexios just fifteen years before – was shown into a room filled from floor to ceiling with objects of gold and silver and fine cloth. Alexios sent presents to the knights and gold coins into the crusaders' camp for distribution to the rank and file. He also insisted that they swear an oath of loyalty to him and promise to hand over any land they took from the Turks that had once been under his rule. Several of the princes were reluctant to take the oath but in the end all but one swore their allegiance. Raymond of Toulouse would only swear that he would never harm the Emperor or deprive him of his rightful possessions.

Above all, Alexios wanted to preserve Constantinople from Turkish control and, if possible, to regain land lost since 1071. He never saw this as a Holy War with spiritual rewards. The Greek Church had not developed that idea or any teaching about penance or indulgences. He simply regarded his new allies as yet another army of mercenaries and he was surprised by their enormous numbers and troubled by their ill-discipline. He feared that his rivals might use the Franks to force him off the throne. He therefore arranged that each contingent of crusaders should be quickly shipped across the Bosphorus strait and to the camp at Kibotos on the shores of Asia, just as he had done with the People's Crusade. This time, unlike the People's Crusade, the armies stayed in the camp until, in May 1097, the order finally came to march south into Muslim-held lands.

The Muslim world

The Muslim world in 1097 was a complex social, political and religious patchwork. In theory at least, all Muslims, no matter where they lived, owed allegiance to the Caliph in Baghdad, who claimed to be the sole political and religious leader of Islam. Since 750, the Caliph had been a member of the Abbasid ruling family. By the time of the First Crusade, the Muslim world had broken into different regions and the Caliph had little central control. The lands of the Abbasids had been taken over by the Seljuk Turks in the second half of the eleventh century. The Seljuks allowed the Abbasid Caliph to continue as a figurehead, but all real power passed to a single Seljuk sultan. From 1072 it was Malik Shah.

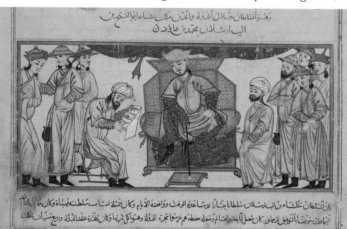

▽ Malik Shah, from a fourteenth-century manuscript. Note the mix of Arabs (in turbans) and Asiatic Turks. They were all Muslims, but with significantly different cultures.

In 1092 both Malik Shah and his chief adviser died suddenly within the space of a few weeks. Disputes broke out in the Sultan's family over who should now rule his lands. These included the Sultanate of Rum, Syria and Palestine, exactly the lands through which the crusaders would march on their way to Jerusalem. As the Sultan's family squabbled, local warlords took the opportunity to build up their own power bases. The Muslim world that the crusaders entered in 1097 was in political chaos.

The situation was made worse by religious divisions. Muslims belong to one of two main groups: **Sunni** and **Shi'ah**. The Seljuks, like the Abbasids, followed the Sunni traditions. In Egypt, however, under a powerful ruling family called the Fatimids, most Muslims were Shi'ite. The Fatimids were keen to extend their power into Seljuk lands, even if it meant fighting against their fellow Muslims. They knew that many poorer Muslims in Syria and Palestine were Shi'ites and would probably prefer Fatimid rule. Caught in the middle were the many Christian and Jewish groups whose ancestors had lived in the region for centuries. In Anatolia, recently taken from the Byzantine Empire, the great majority of people were Christians living under Muslim rule. This 'Muslim world' was highly disjointed. Across the whole region there was no single voice to unify the Muslims against the incoming crusaders. The idea of jihad, which taught that Muslims had a duty to fight to defend Islam, was lying dormant just when Christian belief in Holy War was reaching fever pitch.

Crossing Anatolia: triumph and near disaster

When the crusaders first entered Anatolia (or the Sultanate of Rum as the Seljuks called it) they met little or no resistance. Its ruler, Kilij Arslan, had already ruthlessly defeated the People's Crusade and he underestimated this new force. He made no attempt to attack their camp at Kibotos as they gathered throughout the spring of 1097. He was far away in another part of the sultanate dealing with a rival when the crusaders marched unopposed towards his capital city Nicaea early in May 1097. The crusaders laid siege to the city. On 16 May, Kilij Arslan returned with an army, expecting to wipe out the Franks' force with ease. When he launched his attack, however, his men were so outnumbered that they had to retreat. After holding out for some weeks Nicaea was finally taken by the crusaders on 19 June. Although the Franks were disappointed when Alexios I banned any looting of the city, they were pleased at the cash payments he gave them instead. All was going well: they had defeated the Seljuks in battle and in partnership with their Byzantine allies they had restored to Alexios one of the cities he had lost to the Seljuks years before. The signs looked good for a swift success. Stephen of Blois wrote to his wife to say that he expected the journey to Jerusalem to take five weeks: in reality, it took another two years of intense suffering and near disaster.

The crusader army left Nicaea and set off across central Anatolia. Alexios returned to Constantinople, still fearing a revolution if he left the city for too long. In his place he sent his most loyal general, Tatikios, a half Arab and half Greek eunuch and who – according to some accounts – wore a golden replica nose, his real one having been sliced off in battle! Tatikios joined the council of leading princes that decided strategy. It was a curious way to run a campaign and, as you will discover, rivalry between different princes soon emerged.

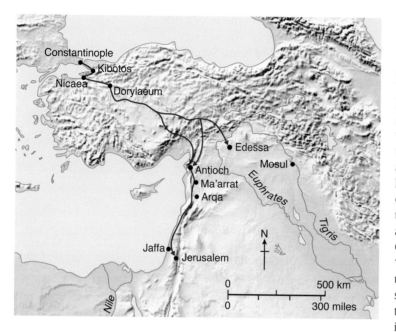

△ **The crusaders' route to Jerusalem.**

On 1 July 1097, as they marched south, a group of 20,000 crusaders had moved ahead of the main army. Unknown to them, the Seljuk leader, Kilij Arslan, had greatly strengthened his forces and was watching closely. Near the town of Dorylaeum he launched a ferocious attack against this leading group. Wave after wave of howling Turkish archers rode to within 60 metres of them and unleashed a hail of arrows. One eyewitness reported that 'to all of us, such warfare was unknown'. It was the military skill of Bohemund that saved the day. He organised the men into a tight defensive formation that held out for over five hours before the main crusader army appeared and forced the Seljuks to flee. At the height of the battle the crusaders encouraged each other with the words 'Stand fast together, trusting in Christ … Today we may gain much booty!' Sure enough, they stripped Kilij Arslan's main camp of gold, silver, food and pack animals. But, as one eyewitness noted, 'If God had not been with us in this battle and sent the other army quickly, none of us would have escaped'.

After the crusaders' successes at Nicaea and Dorylaeum, local Muslim leaders lost faith in the power of Kilij Arslan to defend their communities. One by one the cities of western Anatolia surrendered. The Franks kept their promise to Alexios and returned them to Byzantine control. But the climate and terrain of central Anatolia proved to be a more dangerous enemy: the burning summer sun meant the army could barely cover seven miles a day. Drought and disease took their toll on men and animals: proud knights had to ride oxen or walk carrying their heavy armour in sacks.

For the last part of the crossing, the army split to recover all the former Byzantine lands in southern Anatolia before they pressed on into Syria. Two young lords, Baldwin of Boulogne (younger brother of Godfrey of Bouillon) and Tancred (nephew of Bohemund of Taranto) were such rivals that their armies briefly came to blows as they moved south together. They were both younger members of their family and saw the Crusade as a chance to win fame, status and land. After recapturing the former Byzantine lands, Baldwin and 80 ambitious knights marched east, defeating more Seljuks and liberating Christians from their rule. He may have been motivated purely by selfish greed, or he may have been acting in partnership with Alexios. Either way, by March 1098, Baldwin of Boulogne had become the ruler of the wealthy county of Edessa. He never re-joined the crusader army, but his control of Edessa later proved to be a great help to the success of the First Crusade.

Meanwhile, the rest of the crusader armies regrouped on the borders of Syria and moved south. On 21 October 1097 the greatly reduced force finally reached its next target: the city of Antioch.

■ Check that you have used pages 38 to 40 to add more notes to your table.

From all the notes you have made so far, are you surprised that this Princes' Crusade succeeded in taking Jerusalem?

The siege of Antioch (October 1097 to July 1098)

Stalemate

The crusaders laid siege to Antioch, but the city was well prepared behind its massive walls. The crusaders held their position for months because the rival Seljuk rulers of the Syrian cities of Damascus and Aleppo refused to join forces to remove them. All this led to a lengthy stalemate. After struggling through the blistering heat of the summer, the crusaders now found their tents rotting and stomachs aching in the cold rains of a Syrian winter. Alexios sent them supplies by sea but never enough to meet the crusaders' needs. Expeditions foraged up to 50 miles away for food, sometimes suffering heavy casualties and returning empty-handed. Starvation and disease killed thousands. Thousands more deserted.

In January 1098 Bishop Adhemar, Pope Urban II's representative decided that the stalemate was caused by the army's sinfulness. He called on the crusaders to pray and fast and ordered all women to leave the crusaders' camps so that there should be no sexual activity. He urged wealthier crusaders to give alms, creating a fund from which the needs of the poor could be met. The princes swore publicly that they would never desert the mission. There was more encouragement when a fleet from the Italian port of Genoa arrived nearby, along with reinforcements from as far away as England and Denmark. Morale lifted and religious conviction intensified. It shaped the whole Crusade from this point onwards.

In February 1098 Tatikios and his Byzantine troops left the siege to find Alexios and persuade him to send help. They never returned. In that same month, despite being greatly outnumbered, the remaining crusaders fought off a Muslim relief army that had at last been sent by the Seljuk ruler of Aleppo. Their numbers may have dropped but the crusaders' commitment and skill at dealing with the Seljuk style of fighting was increasing. In April, however, the crusaders learned that an even larger

△ Antioch's walls are obvious in this nineteenth century print of the city. The walls are over six miles in length and the crusaders could not patrol them to stop supplies reaching the city during their siege.

■ Start your fourth table, based on the one on page 33. This time, use the heading 'The siege of Antioch'.

41

Muslim relief force was on its way to Antioch. It was led by Kerbogha, the ruler of the distant city of Mosul, who wanted to extend his power into Syria. He formed alliances with others who hoped to displace local Seljuk rulers. By May 1098, Kerbogha's force was approaching Antioch and the crusader army faced the possibility of being trapped and destroyed outside the city if it could not break into Antioch and shelter behind its walls. Faced with this new crisis, many more crusaders deserted.

Breakthrough

In the princes' council, Bohemund argued that Alexios had failed to fulfil his duties and this freed them from their promise to return all Byzantine lands to him. He said he knew how to take Antioch but that he wanted to keep the city for himself if his plan should succeed. Despite the reluctance of Raymond of Toulouse, the princes agreed. Stephen of Blois was not convinced that they could take the city. A month earlier he had written to his wife that he was sure that the souls of crusaders killed in battle went directly to heaven as the Pope had promised – but he clearly was not keen to find out for himself if it was really true. On the night of 2 June he and his knights deserted. To make matters worse, two weeks later as he fled north, Stephen met Emperor Alexios I who was making his way towards Antioch with reinforcements. Stephen told Alexios that the city was doomed and the Emperor turned back. But, unknown to them, just 24 hours after Stephen of Blois fled, the city had fallen to the crusaders.

Bohemund had secretly made contact with a Christian inside Antioch who commanded a tower on the city walls. He bribed his contact to betray his Muslim masters. On the night of 2 June this man silently lowered a rope from the walls. A small group of knights climbed over and opened a main gate. The crusaders poured into the city crying 'God wills it!' and set about a brutal massacre of the Muslim population. Only the **citadel**, high on the cliffs above the main city, held out against the crusaders. By the morning of 4 June the rest of Antioch was in Christian hands. But by the end of that same day, the army of Kerbogha arrived: the crusaders were safe, but trapped inside the city.

Victory against all the odds

Difficult as this situation was it could have been worse. Kerbogha's army had been delayed and diverted by Baldwin's knights near Edessa. Without this, Kerbogha might have arrived in time to crush the Christian armies outside the city walls. As it was, he now had them trapped within Antioch. The spirits of the crusaders fell and once again many, mostly unarmed pilgrims, made their escape through latrines or over the walls at night. By this time only about 25,000 of the original force of about 50,000 were left.

Then came a remarkable change.

One night, just when the desertions reached their peak, a poor crusader, Peter Bartholomew, declared that God had shown him where they would find the remnants of the lance that a Roman soldier used to pierce the side of Christ on the cross. Sure enough, on 14 June, Peter led the princes to a spot in Antioch's cathedral where, under the stone floor, he dug up a fragment of what appeared to be an ancient spear. Some crusaders were not convinced, but others such as Raymond of Toulouse took this as a sign from God. Whatever the object was, its discovery changed the mood of the crusader army not just at Antioch but for the rest of the expedition. From that point onwards there were regular reports of visions and signs from God and the religious fervour of the crusaders intensified. After some days of prayer and fasting, despite being heavily outnumbered, they dared to launch an extraordinary counter attack against Kerbogha's army.

On 28 June the main gates of Antioch swung open and a tight knit formation of knights and infantry marched out under the expert direction of Bohemund and with Bishop Adhemar carrying the 'holy lance'. Almost all were on foot, but at least one German knight rode a donkey so small that his feet dragged along the ground! Catching the Muslims by surprise, the crusaders easily crossed a bridge that should have been better defended and they quickly engaged Kerbogha's first line of troops in hand-to-hand combat. When Kerbogha's allies saw the front line crumbling, many deserted him and he too turned and fled. Very soon the crusaders were looting his camp for riches and food, executing every single Muslim they caught. Seeing all this, the citadel in Antioch soon surrendered.

Once again – and not surprisingly – the crusaders thanked God for their victory. Some claimed to have seen a host of saints on white horses fighting alongside them in the heat of the battle. The first Christian accounts of the victory say the army was inspired by its belief in the power of the 'holy lance', but there is evidence that the princes had tried to negotiate a surrender in the days before this battle and had promised Kerbogha that they would return to Europe if he would spare their lives. He rejected their plea and left them with no alternative but to fight to the death. It may have been fear and desperation, as much as faith and inspiration, which drove the crusaders to their unlikely victory at Antioch.

> ■ Check that you have used pages 41 to 43 to add more notes to your table.
>
> From all the notes you have made so far, are you surprised that this Princes' Crusade succeeded in taking Jerusalem?

Antioch to Jerusalem (August 1098 to August 1099)

Disputes and delays

After the victory at Antioch, the rank and file crusaders urged their leaders to march directly to Jerusalem but the princes fell into squabbling. Bohemund, sure that he was now the rightful ruler of Antioch, made trade agreements with Genoese sailors who were eager to gain material rewards from the crusaders' success. Raymond of Toulouse argued that the city should be handed to Alexios but he probably wanted it for himself. As the princes feuded, some knights went to serve Baldwin in Edessa, while others rode off to win more land from the Seljuks in northern Syria. The Crusade was losing its way. To make matters worse, Bishop Adhemar, whose leadership had once revived the Crusade, died on 1 August 1098.

The princes now sent Hugh of Vermandois back to Constantinople to persuade Alexios to come and lead the Crusade in person, but the Emperor refused. He still feared a revolution if he left his capital. From this moment the Franks believed Alexios had given up on them and felt that any land they took would be their own. The princes invited Pope Urban II to come and lead the march to Jerusalem but he too refused. No one was taking the lead in the final stage of the Crusade.

> ■ Start your final table, based on the one on page 33. This time, use the heading 'Antioch to Jerusalem'.

The feud between Bohemund and Raymond grew worse and only the pleas of most of the troops stopped the two men coming to blows. Ties of loyalty were breaking and knights shifted their allegiance depending on who might reward them best. Raymond of Toulouse offered something like a transfer fee of thousands of gold coins to win over two of Bohemund's supporters, Robert of Normandy and Tancred. As if to compete with Bohemund, Raymond captured the city of Ma'arrat and made it his base. Without unified leadership, the focus on Jerusalem was rapidly disappearing.

The map on page 40 shows the crusaders' route from Antioch to Jerusalem.

It was the rank and file who forced the issue. Early in January 1099 a crowd of poor Franks began tearing down the walls of Ma'arrat. They were telling Raymond that this was no time to be settling in northern Syria: he had to take the lead and march on to Jerusalem. The men's determination to press on may have been driven by their desire to fulfil their crusader vows or simply by their desperate hunger. So short were supplies at Ma'arrat that some crusaders even resorted to eating the flesh of their Muslim victims. Raymond repented and agreed to lead his 7000 men south to take Jerusalem. Within weeks the forces of Godfrey of Bouillon and Robert of Flanders joined in and Bohemund also sent men from his own army. The diagram below shows how numbers fell over two years.

c. 50,000 — Constantinople May 1097

c. 25,000 — Antioch May 1098

c. 14,000 — Jerusalem June 1099

The first weeks of 1099 saw the crusaders moving south through Syria and into Palestine. Many cities either surrendered or simply allowed them to pass unchallenged as they had heard of the crusaders' ferocity. Besides, many Syrians were Shi'ites who resented being ruled by the Sunni Seljuks. But in mid February progress stalled and the reputation of Raymond of Toulouse fell once again. He held up the march to Jerusalem by laying siege to the city of Arqa and the soldiers believed he was once again looking to create a new land base for himself. Raymond also lost credibility by his support for Peter Bartholomew. Since his discovery of the 'holy lance' in June 1098, Peter had continued to have visions but these became less and less convincing. In April 1099 he volunteered to test his honesty by walking barefoot over red hot coals: only if he survived this ordeal would he be accepted as God's messenger. Peter did survive … but only for a few days. With his death, power shifted from Raymond towards Godfrey of Bouillon, who had always wanted to press on to Jerusalem. He could also feed and equip his followers effectively as his brother Baldwin sent regular supplies from Edessa.

In July 1098, the Fatimids based in Egypt, had taken Jerusalem from their Muslim rivals, the Seljuks. When the city's new rulers heard that the crusaders were approaching, they asked Cairo to send reinforcements. Godfrey persuaded the crusaders that they must reach Jerusalem quickly, before the Fatimid reinforcements could arrive. The crusader armies marched south again but not without more disputes as Tancred and Raymond squabbled over who should become Lord of Bethlehem.

The capture of Jerusalem

On 7 June the 14,000 crusaders at last arrived at the walls of Jerusalem. Some walked the last few miles barefoot as pilgrims. In another sign of disunity, the army split with Godfrey's forces to the north and Raymond's to the south, and the two groups barely communicated. For four weeks they camped in the burning sun, preparing their attack. Genoese sailors carried timbers from their own ships at Jaffa on the coast, so that their carpenters could make siege towers to help the crusaders climb over the walls into the city. The Muslims simply strengthened their defences at the points where they could see the siege towers and waited for help from Cairo.

Then, in early July, just as at Antioch, prompted by a poor pilgrim's vision from God, the crusaders fasted and confessed their sins. On 8 July after processing around the walls of the city, they gathered on a mountainside and the leaders publicly buried their differences.

At dawn on 14 July 1099 the crusaders launched their assault. During the battle some reported seeing the dead Bishop Adhemar fighting beside them, while others believed St George stood on a nearby hillside, waving his shield and showing them where to attack. The masterstroke came from Godfrey of Bouillon who dismantled a siege tower overnight and rebuilt it at a point where the defences were weak. He climbed over the walls, opened the gates and allowed the crusaders to enter the Holy City and begin their bloodthirsty massacre of its inhabitants. One reported that:

> Our men rushed around the whole city, seizing gold and silver, horses and mules and houses full of all sorts of goods, and they all came rejoicing and weeping from excess of gladness to worship at the Holy Sepulchre of our Saviour Jesus where they fulfilled their vows.

For more on the crusaders' capture of Jerusalem see the Insight on pages 48 and 49.

At sunrise on 15 July the new day dawned with Jerusalem under Christian control for the first time since 638. Exactly two weeks later, far away in Rome, Pope Urban II died. The man whose sermon had set in motion these extraordinary events never knew of the crusaders' triumph.

The aftermath of victory

The princes decided to create a new kingdom of Jerusalem and, on 22 July, the crown was offered to Raymond of Toulouse who was the most senior lord and who wished to remain in the east. But to the surprise of all, he refused the offer, suggesting that no one should be called king where Jesus had worn the crown of thorns. He may have done this for genuine religious reasons or he may have thought Jerusalem was too small a kingdom for his ambitions. Whatever the reasons, the crown went instead to Godfrey of Bouillon. He too insisted that he would not use the title 'king' but he quickly assumed control.

On 12 August 1099, Godfrey's army of 10,000 crusaders caught the Fatimid relief force unprepared on the coast near Ascalon. The element of surprise, the well-rehearsed battle tactics, his own decisive leadership and above all the hard-won unity of purpose amongst the mass of the crusaders brought a swift victory. Muslims fled in disarray, some hiding in trees only to be shot down without mercy by Christian archers. It is a fitting symbol of the weakness of the Muslim defence of their lands.

■ Events after the capture of Jerusalem also help us to decide if the capture of the city was a surprising achievement. Be sure to keep adding notes to your final table based on this account.

Almost immediately after the battle at Ascalon, the vast majority of the crusaders began their journey home. Many carried palm fronds, the traditional sign of the pilgrim returning from Jerusalem. Others took religious relics of great value, but it is hard to say whether this represents greed or piety. Our twenty-first-century minds tend to divide religious devotion and material wealth. To most crusaders this distinction meant nothing: they saw wealth as a sign of God's blessing. That would certainly be true of the merchants from Genoa who proudly took the bones of John the Baptist from Antioch back to Italy as they praised God for victory and looked forward to years of rich trade with the newly Christian lands in the east.

Even the poorest of the crusaders were paid a good sum in cash for their part in the final attack on Jerusalem. Their influence on the Crusade had grown in its final year and they could not be ignored. But, by then, thousands had already deserted. Many more had died in battle or from starvation or disease. We know little or nothing about these people and what made them join the Crusade. They must have been an extraordinary mixture, but it seems likely that for most of them this had not been an attempt to win land or property and it was their hope of an easier passage to heaven that drove them on.

As for the leaders, here is what happened to them:

Bishop Adhemar	Was buried in Antioch cathedral in the precise place where the 'holy lance' had been dug up (August 1098).
Robert of Normandy	Returned to Europe and challenged his brother for the throne of England. He failed and lived the last twenty years of his life as a prisoner.
Robert of Flanders	Went home to win fame as 'Robert of Jerusalem'. He took with him the arm of St George. He built a monastery … and carried on making war.
Godfrey of Bouillon	Established and enlarged the kingdom of Jerusalem but died in July 1100. He was buried in the Church of the Holy Sepulchre, just yards from where it was believed Christ's own body had been laid to rest.
Baldwin of Edessa	Continued to rule as Count of Edessa and also became King of Jerusalem in 1100 on the death of his brother Godfrey.
Raymond of Toulouse	Eventually won the land he wanted by taking the port of Lattakiah from his old rival Bohemund. He gradually won more land along the coast. When he died in 1105 this became the County of Tripoli.
Bohemund of Taranto	Continued as ruler of Antioch and attempted to spread his territory. Aided by his nephew Tancred, he even made war against the Emperor Alexios. He died in 1111.
Hugh of Vermandois	After being sent to seek help from Alexios in 1098, Hugh simply continued back to France. He joined a third wave of crusaders who tried but failed to win more Muslim land in 1101 and died in battle.
Stephen of Blois	Returned home after deserting at Antioch. His wife sent him back to the Holy Land where he died fighting against the Muslims in 1102.

As the chart shows, war against the Muslims continued after the capture of Jerusalem as Christians fought with limited success to take more land in the east. In the case of Bohemund, his armies tried to take more land from the Byzantine Empire. The Byzantines were furious and the alliance between Latin Christians and Greek Christians would never regain the strength that had been established between Urban II and Alexios I in 1095.

◼ Concluding your enquiry

By now you will have gathered all sorts of evidence about the crusaders' motivation and leadership and Muslim opposition. It's time to review this evidence and reach an informed conclusion. The grid below should help.

For each factor:

a) Use the notes in your tables to consider all the questions raised in the left-hand column. (And try to think of other questions.)

b) In the light of your answers to the questions on the left, decide where along the line you would place a mark to show what you have decided. The mark would be towards the left if you think that factor made success likely. If you think it made success unlikely and therefore surprising, the mark would be towards the right.

c) For each factor (crusaders' motivations, crusaders' leadership, Muslim opposition), write a single paragraph that sums up your conclusion and supports it with details you have gathered in your note tables.

d) After summarising your ideas on each factor, write another paragraph summarising your overall answer to our original question: Should we be surprised by the success of the First Crusade?

Issues to consider:	Your overall conclusion about each factor	
	Made success likely	Made success surprising
Crusaders' motivation • What did motivate the crusaders? • Did religious motivation matter more than the desire to gain wealth and land? • Did it matter that different crusaders had different motives? • Did desertions hinder or help the Crusade? • At what point would you say the crusaders were at the peak of their motivation?	⟵――――――――――――――――⟶	
Crusaders' leadership • Was the model of leadership used in the Crusade helpful in any way? • Who (if anyone) emerges as an effective crusader leader? How? When? Why? • Who (if anyone) emerges as a weak crusader leader? How? When? Why?	⟵――――――――――――――――⟶	
Muslim opposition • When (if ever) did the Muslims mount an effective opposition to the First Crusade? • When (if ever) was the Muslim opposition particularly ineffective? • What best explains any weaknesses in Muslim opposition to the First Crusade?	⟵――――――――――――――――⟶	

The massacre at Jerusalem in 1099

How do historians write about controversial events?

The Christians' sacking of Jerusalem in 1099 was shocking at the time and has retained or even increased its notoriety ever since. When writing about highly charged and sensitive matters like this, a real challenge confronts historians. They must:

- establish and communicate the facts without being too remote and analytical about human suffering
- capture the drama and intensity without indulging in gratuitous details of violence
- show that their account is based on critical, fair-minded use of sources
- show an understanding of the wider context of the event in its time without making excuses for inhuman behaviour
- use language carefully, showing where there are ambiguities and doubts without constantly sitting on the fence.

Here are two recent accounts of the crusaders' sacking of Jerusalem in July 1099. They are from histories of the Crusades written in 2006 and 2010 by historians Christopher Tyerman and Thomas Asbridge. Compare the way they tackle the challenges listed above.

From Christopher Tyerman, *God's Warriors* (2006)

The massacre in Jerusalem spared few. Jews were burned inside their synagogue. Muslims were indiscriminately cut to pieces, decapitated or slowly tortured by fire (this on Christian evidence). Such was the scale and horror of the carnage that one Jewish witness was reduced to noticing approvingly that at least the Christians did not rape their victims before killing them as Muslims did. The city was comprehensively ransacked: gold, silver, horses, food, the domestic contents of houses, were seized by the conquerors in a pillage as thorough as any in the Middle Ages ... The city's narrow streets were clogged with corpses and dismembered body parts, including some crusaders crushed in their zeal for the pursuit and massacre of the defenders. The heaps of dead presented an immediate problem for the conquerors; on 17 July many of the surviving Muslim population were forced to clear the streets and carry the bodies outside the walls to be burnt in great pyres, whereat they themselves were massacred, a chilling pre-echo of later genocidal practices.

This secondary slaughter, in cold blood, perhaps even more than the initial mayhem, provoked mounting retrospective shock and outrage amongst the Muslim intellectuals, religious leaders and politicians over the next century and a half. Some thousands, men, women and children, were massacred, although certainly fewer than the 70,000 trumpeted in early thirteenth-century Arabic chronicles. A few Muslim and Jewish Jerusalemites survived, managing either to escape ... or to be ransomed, a process that could take months, suggesting a not entirely indiscriminate policy of killing on the part of the crusaders. Massacres were not a monopoly of western Christians. The recent Turkish conquests in the Near East had been accompanied by carnage and enslavement on a grand scale. When it suited, Muslim victors could behave as bestially as any Christian, as Zengi showed at Edessa in 1144 and Saladin was to prove in suppressing opposition in Egypt in the 1170s and in the killing of the knights in the military orders after the battle of Hattin in 1187. Immediate contemporary Muslim reaction appeared muted when contrasted to later polemics. Massacres as well as atrocity stories were – and are – an inescapable part of war. In the face of a Muslim counter-attack, letting the locals live may not have seemed a prudent option to the Christian victors, however obscene the alternative.

From Thomas Asbridge, *The Crusades* (2010)

Surging through the streets in blood-hungry, ravening packs, they overran the Holy City. What little Muslim resistance remained melted away before them, but most Franks were in no mood to take prisoners. Instead, three years of strife, privation and yearning coalesced to fuel a rampaging torrent of barbaric and indiscriminate slaughter … A Latin eyewitness described how 'all the defenders retreated along the walls and through the city, and our men went after them, killing them and cutting them down as far as the [Aqsa Mosque], where there was such a massacre that our men were wading up to their ankles in enemy blood'. Tancred gave his banner to a group huddled on the roof of the Aqsa, designating them as his captives, but even they were later slain in cold blood by other Franks. So gruesome was the carnage that, according to one Latin, 'even the soldiers who were carrying out the killing could hardly bear the vapours from the warm blood'. Other crusaders ranged through the city at will, slaughtering men, women and children, both Muslims and Jews, all the while engaging in rapacious looting.
Neither Latin nor Arabic sources shy away from recording the dreadful horror of this sack, the one side glorying in victory, the other appalled by its raw savagery. In the decades that followed Near East Islam came to regard the Latin atrocities at Jerusalem as an act of crusader barbarity and defilement, demanding of urgent vengeance. By the thirteenth century, the Iraqi Muslim Ibn al-Athir estimated the number of Muslim dead at 70,000. Modern historians long regarded this figure to be an exaggeration, but generally accepted the Latin estimates in excess of 10,000 might be accurate. However, recent research has uncovered close contemporary Hebrew testimony which indicates that casualties may not have exceeded 3,000, and that large numbers of prisoners were taken when Jerusalem fell. This suggests that, even in the Middle Ages, the image of the crusaders' brutality in 1099 was subject to hyperbole and manipulation on both sides of the divide.
Even so, we must still acknowledge the terrible inhumanity of the crusaders' sadistic butchery … The Frankish massacre was not simply a feral outburst of bottled rage; it was a prolonged, callous campaign of killing that lasted at least two days and it left the city awash with blood and littered with corpses. In the midsummer heat the stench soon became intolerable, and the dead were dragged out beyond the city walls, 'piled up in mounds as big as houses' and burned. Even six months later a Latin visiting Palestine for the first time commented that the Holy City still reeked of death and decay.

4 What can particular sources reveal about the crusader states?

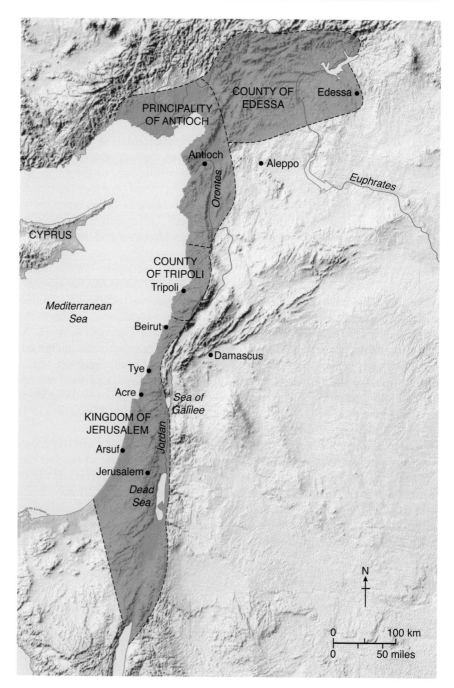

COUNTY OF EDESSA

Edessa

PRINCIPALITY OF ANTIOCH

Antioch

Aleppo

Euphrates

Orontes

CYPRUS

COUNTY OF TRIPOLI

Tripoli

Mediterranean Sea

Beirut

Damascus

Tye

Acre

Sea of Galilee

KINGDOM OF JERUSALEM

Jordan

Arsuf

Jerusalem

Dead Sea

N

0   100 km
0   50 miles

▷ The crusader states in the early twelfth century. Although the map shows clear political boundaries for the crusader states, no definite borders existed at that time.

In the first decades of the twelfth century the Franks captured most of the Mediterranean seaports and created the four 'crusader states' that you can see on the map opposite: the Kingdom of Jerusalem, the principality of Antioch and the counties of Tripoli and Edessa. For nearly 200 years the crusading movement was dominated by the need to settle and preserve these isolated and vulnerable states. During the twelfth century, the Franks' attempts to expand eastwards were unsuccessful and the cities of Aleppo and Damascus always remained in Muslim hands. In 1144, it was the eastern state of Edessa that was the first to fall to the Muslims. From the 1160s the Kingdom of Jerusalem came under increasing threat from Muslim forces. In 1291, when the Muslims recaptured Acre, the crusader states collapsed completely.

In the Middle Ages the land that the Franks sought to control in the Near East was sometimes known as **Outremer**, the land beyond the sea. From north to south the territory stretched for about 800 miles. In area, it was roughly the same size as England. You can see that the region was dominated by mountains and hills. To the west of the high land there was a narrow coastal plain and in the east the land flattened into treeless scrub and desert. Much of the land, particularly the coastal strip, was agriculturally rich and the inhabitants produced cereals, sugar cane, fruit and vegetables. Many people were also involved in trade. They lived and worked in the seaports of Acre, Tyre, Beirut and Tripoli eagerly awaiting caravans of camels carrying silks, spices and dyes from the great Syrian trading cities of Damascus and Aleppo.

■ **Enquiry Focus:** What can particular sources reveal about the crusader states?

This enquiry focuses on two issues relating to the crusader states in the first half of the twelfth century:

a) the formation and survival of the crusader states

b) the ways in which Muslims and Christians related to each other within these states.

The way in which the crusaders established their authority over the territory, and the nature of the society that emerged in the crusader states during the twelfth century, are issues that have caused heated historical debate. Over time, historians have suggested three very different models:

1 **The 'assimilation' model.** In the mid nineteenth-century French historians drew parallels between the relationship between France and its colonies and the nature of society in the twelfth-century crusader states. They were keen to emphasise the good relations that existed between the Franks and the inhabitants of the occupied countries. These historians characterised crusader society as a 'melting pot' in which westerners mingled harmoniously with the indigenous population of eastern Christians and Muslims to produce a society that was culturally unique.

2 **The 'segregation' model.** The 'assimilation' model was challenged in the 1950s and 60s – a time of anti-colonialism. Some historians in Britain and Israel argued that the crusader states were a segregated society in which the Franks were an oppressive and dominating elite. These historians suggested that the westerners lived in a few heavily defended towns and fortresses, segregated themselves from the indigenous population and used military force as a method of domination. In other words, they created a kind of 'medieval apartheid'.

3 The 'messy mixture' model. In recent years, the research of historians, archaeologists, historical geographers and art historians has helped us to develop a much more complex understanding of the crusader states. Their work suggests that a 'messy mixture' of assimilation and segregation is likely to be closer to reality.

This enquiry introduces you to some of the sources that historians have used to investigate how the crusader states were formed and the nature of crusader society that emerged in the first half of the twelfth century. We have selected six fascinating sources relating mainly to the Kingdom of Jerusalem. Each source sheds some light on specific issues relating to the formation of the crusader states and the nature of crusader society.

Source	Specific issues
Chronicle of Fulcher of Chartres, c. 1120.	The reign of Baldwin I and the formation of the Kingdom of Jerusalem, 1100–18
Al-Sulami's *Book of Holy War*, 1105	The initial Muslim response to the First Crusade and the formation of the crusader states
William of Tyre's *Historia*, 1184	The formation of the Order of Knights Templar in 1118
Queen Melisende's Psalter, 1143	Political power in the Kingdom of Jerusalem and the nature of crusader art
The site of Castellum Regis	Crusader settlement in the first half of the eleventh century
Usama ibn Munqidh's *Book of Contemplation*, 1180s	Relations between Franks and Muslims in the 1140s

As you work through the six sections of the enquiry you will find it helpful to make a 'source summary' for each of the sources you study. Divide each source summary into three sections based on the following:

1 The background to the source: What is it? Who produced it? When? Why? What do historians need to bear in mind when using the source?
2 An explanation of what the particular source reveals about a specific aspect of the crusader states.
3 A summary of the wider issues relating to the formation of the crusader states and the nature of crusader society that you discover in each section.

At the end of the enquiry you should use your source summaries to:

a) explain how the crusader states were formed in the first decades of the twelfth century
b) describe the nature of the society that emerged in the crusader states.

Source summary

1. Background

2. What source reveals

3. Wider issues

Fulcher of Chartres' chronicle

Fulcher of Chartres was a 40-year-old priest in northern France when he joined the First Crusade in 1096. At Antioch in 1097, Fulcher was appointed as chaplain to Baldwin of Boulogne, one of the leaders of the crusade. When Baldwin was crowned King of Jerusalem in 1100, Fulcher became royal chaplain and he lived in Jerusalem until 1127. It was there that Fulcher of Chartres wrote *A History of the Expedition to Jerusalem, 1095–1127* – his chronicle of the First Crusade and the reigns of Baldwin I and Baldwin II. Fulcher was an eyewitness to many of the events in his chronicle and his work is considered to be reliable in many respects. However, we have to remember that Fulcher's relationship with Baldwin I may have influenced his writing and that his chronicle may also have been shaped by his desire to attract settlers to the crusader states.

You have already studied one extract from Fulcher of Chartres' chronicle on page 30.

◁ The inhabitants of Edessa pay homage to Baldwin I. A miniature in William of Tyre, *Historia Rerum in Partibus Transmarinis Gestarum*, thirteenth century.

This picture, from a thirteenth-century Christian manuscript, shows Baldwin of Boulogne receiving tribute from Christians and Muslims in Edessa. During the First Crusade Baldwin had broken away from the other leaders to establish his own independent lordship. Through clever political manoeuvring and brutal conquest Baldwin had seized control of the city of Edessa and the neighbouring territory. This became the first crusader state in the Near East – the county of Edessa. In September 1100, messengers arrived in Edessa and presented Baldwin with a stunning opportunity to further enhance his power. Following the death of Godfrey of Bouillon, Baldwin's older brother and first crusading ruler of Jerusalem, Baldwin was invited to be the new ruler of the Kingdom of Jerusalem. Fulcher of Chartres wrote in his chronicle that Baldwin 'grieved somewhat at the death of his brother, but rejoiced more over his inheritance'.

See page 40 for Baldwin's rise to power in Edessa.

■ What impression are you beginning to form of Baldwin I?

Baldwin's challenge

In October 1100, Baldwin left Edessa with just 200 knights and 700 infantrymen. He marched south to Jerusalem, defeating a Muslim army from Damascus on the way and, on 9 November, arrived in Jerusalem to the cheers of Latin, Greek and Syrian Christians. Baldwin's brother, Godfrey of Bouillon, had refused to title himself 'King of Jerusalem' believing that only Christ could be king of the Holy City. But Baldwin had no such scruples. On Christmas Day 1100, in the Church of the Nativity in Bethlehem, Baldwin was crowned and anointed with the title King of Jerusalem. The task that lay ahead of him was immense. In 1100, the Franks held only a few outposts scattered across the Kingdom of Jerusalem. Over the next few years Baldwin I would have to expand and consolidate his lands in the face of fierce Muslim opposition.

In his chronicle, Fulcher of Chartres leaves us in no doubt as to the enormity of the challenge facing Baldwin I in the early stages of the formation of the Kingdom of Jerusalem:

> In the beginning of his reign Baldwin as yet possessed few cities and people. He was a very skilful fighter and so, although he had few men, they [the Muslims] did not dare to attack him. Up to 1100 the land route was completely blocked to our pilgrims. Meanwhile, French as well as English, or Italians and Venetians, came by sea as far as Jaffa. At first we had no other port. These pilgrims came very timidly in single ships, or in squadrons of three or four, through the midst of hostile pirates and past the ports of the **Saracens**. They came on to Jerusalem; they visited the Holy of Holies, for which purpose they had come. Some remained in the Holy Land and others went back. For this reason the land of Jerusalem remained depopulated. There were not enough people to defend it from the Saracens if only the latter dared attack us. We did not at that time have 300 knights and as many footmen to defend Jerusalem, Jaffa, Ramla and the stronghold of Haifa. We scarcely dared to assemble our knights when we wished to plan some feat. We feared that in the meantime they would do some damage against our deserted fortifications. It was a miracle that we lived amongst so many thousands and thousands [of Muslims] as their conquerors, made some of them our tributaries and ruined others by plundering them and making them captives. Our power came from the Almighty. Often indeed we were sad when we could get no aid from our friends across the sea. We were in need of nothing if only men and horses did not fail us. The men who came by sea to Jerusalem could not bring horses with them, and no-one came to help us by land. The people of Antioch were not able to help neither us, nor we them.

■ What does this extract from the chronicle of Fulcher of Chartres reveal about the particular challenges facing Baldwin I in the early stages of the formation of the Kingdom of Jerusalem?

Begin a source summary for Fulcher of Chartres' chronicle. (Check the instructions in the Enquiry Focus on pages 51 and 52.)

Baldwin's battles

In the early years of his reign, Baldwin's priorities were the conquest of the coastal ports and the defence of the south of his kingdom against Fatimid forces from Egypt. In 1101, the King, with help from the Genoese fleet, captured the port of Arsuf. When the Muslim population asked for peace Baldwin allowed them to leave the city with their goods. At Caesarea, twenty-odd miles to the north, the Muslim population were not so fortunate. The **emir** of Caesarea, hoping for help from the Fatimids, refused to surrender. In response, Baldwin's troops killed most of the male population, enslaved the women and children, and plundered the town. Some of Baldwin's men even burned piles of corpses in order to find the gold coins that people had swallowed. In 1104 when Baldwin besieged the important port of Acre it is not surprising that its inhabitants soon surrendered. Baldwin allowed them to remain in Acre in return for payment of a poll tax. This extract from the chronicle of Fulcher of Chartres sheds some further light on the siege:

For more details on the Fatimids, see page 16.

> In 1104 Baldwin laid siege to Acre. Just at that time a fleet from Genoa had arrived at Syria and Baldwin sent a message to the fleet inviting them in a friendly way to fight for Christ before going home. Through able and shrewd mediators an agreement was reached. On condition that they should be given in perpetuity a third part of the returns and revenues collected at the port of Acre from sea imports and in addition be granted a Church and full jurisdiction over one street, the Genoese consented to lend royal aid in taking the city. They blockaded it whilst the King laid siege on land. After 20 days they [the inhabitants of Acre] surrendered. Thus for the first time a safe and convenient approach was opened to those arriving by sea.

■ What does the extract reveal about the way in which Baldwin established his authority in the Kingdom of Jerusalem?

Add more details to your source summary.

Baldwin's kingdom

Baldwin was almost constantly at war throughout the remainder of his reign. In 1105, 1107 and 1111 he confronted further Egyptian attacks from the south. Between 1109 and 1115 he was occupied in the north where a combined Muslim force from Mosul and Damascus attacked his kingdom. After 1115 he established his authority in the region to the south of the Dead Sea in order to control the trade routes between Egypt and Syria. As his realm became more secure, Baldwin was careful to ensure that the balance of power in the Kingdom of Jerusalem lay with the king and not with his nobility. He built up a powerful royal domain, ensuring that important settlements such as Jerusalem, Jaffa and Acre were owned and administered directly by the crown. Baldwin created few new lordships for his barons, preferring to reward them with money fiefs. This ensured that his barons had limited territorial power.

Baldwin I succeeded in creating a loyal aristocracy that was subservient to the crown, but the barons could still flex their muscles when it came to the issue of succession. Baldwin was married but failed to produce an heir. There are some suggestions in the medieval sources that Baldwin was a homosexual. In 1118 Baldwin mounted his final campaign against

The royal domain was the land owned and administered directly by the crown. A money fief was a grant of land that did not include the right of ownership and inheritance.

the Fatimids of Egypt. It was during this raid on the Nile that one of his old war wounds re-opened. He never recovered and died on his journey back to Jerusalem. The barons acted decisively, electing the King's cousin as Baldwin II, King of Jerusalem. As this final extract from the chronicle of Fulcher of Chartres makes clear, the kingdom that Baldwin II now ruled was very different from the one his cousin had inherited in 1100.

'Occidentals' means westerners. 'Orientals' means easterners.

■ What does this extract reveal about crusader society in the 1120s?

Why do you think historians should be wary of taking Fulcher of Chartres' description at face value (see page 53)?

Complete your source summary for Fulcher of Chartres' chronicle.

Consider, I pray, and reflect how in our time God has transferred the West into the East, for we who are Occidentals have now been made Orientals. He who was a Roman or a Frank is now a Galilean, or an inhabitant of Palestine. One who was a citizen of Rheims or of Chartres now has been made a citizen of Tyre or Antioch. We have already forgotten the places of our birth; already they have become unknown to many of us, or, at least, are unmentioned. Some already possess here homes and servants which they have received through inheritance. Some have taken wives not merely of their own people, but Syrians, or **Armenians**, or even Saracens who have received the grace of baptism. Some have with them father-in-law, or daughter-in-law, or son-in-law, or stepson or step-father. There are here, too, grandchildren and great-grandchildren. One cultivates vines, another fields. The one and the other use mutually the speech and the idioms of the different languages, now made common, become known to both races, and faith unites those whose forefathers were strangers. As it is written, 'the lion and the ox shall eat straw together'. Those who were strangers are now natives; and he who was a sojourner has become a resident. Our parents and relatives from day to day come to join us, abandoning, even though reluctantly, all that they possess. For those who were poor there, here God makes rich.

Al-Sulami's *Book of Holy War*

Fulcher of Chartres was puzzled by the lack of a united attack on the crusader states from Muslim forces. In his chronicle he asked 'why did they not, as innumerable locusts in a little field, so completely devour and destroy us?' This was a vivid image from someone who had experienced at least three plagues of locusts during his time in Jerusalem. We have seen that Baldwin I faced fierce opposition from different Muslim forces, but at the beginning of the twelfth century, the Muslims of the Near East were divided. There was no unified Muslim reaction to the First Crusade or to the emerging crusader states. Hardly anyone in the early twelfth century called for a collective response to the Frankish invasion of the Holy Land. Al-Sulami, a jurist from Damascus, was the exception.

See pages 38–39 on Muslim disunity.

Al-Sulami taught at the magnificent Great Mosque in Damascus, constructed by the Umayyads in the early eighth century. Around 1105, al-Sulami delivered a number of public lectures from the elaborately carved minbar (pulpit) in the Great Mosque. He recorded his thoughts in a treatise, *Kitab al-Jihad* (*Book of Holy War*), parts of which still survive. They provide a rare insight into the thinking of a Muslim religious leader

in the early twelfth century. Al-Sulami called for jihad – Holy War. Jihad had been part of the Islamic faith from its foundation in the seventh century. 'Greater' jihad was the personal struggle of the individual against immorality and sin. 'Lesser' jihad was the obligation on all Muslims to defend Islam through war against unbelievers. Jihad had driven the early expansion of Islam, but from the late eighth century it had declined in importance. Al-Sulami argued that Frankish invasion of Syria and Palestine was God's punishment for the neglect of jihad by Muslim leaders.

Al-Sulami's treatise showed a remarkable understanding of the wider context of the First Crusade. He linked the invasion of Palestine and Syria to the Norman conquest of Islamic Sicily (1060–91) and to the Christian conquest of Islamic Spain. The First Crusade, he argued, was a planned assault that revealed the disunity of the Muslim Near East. Al-Sulami understood the spiritual importance of the conquest of Jerusalem for the Franks and he was unusual in appreciating the religious roots of the western invasion of Palestine and Syria. He also knew that the Franks had succeeded through luck as well as military power. Like Fulcher of Chartres, al-Sulami was aware that the Franks' lack of knights and their weak supply links with Europe made them vulnerable. He argued that a united commitment to jihad from Muslim leaders could drive the Franks out of the Near East.

△ A photograph of the Great Umayyad Mosque of Damascus, where al-Sulami taught in the early twelfth century.

As for consensus, after the death of the Prophet (God bless him) the four caliphs and all the companions of the Prophet agreed on the jihad's being incumbent on all. Not one of them left off prosecuting it during his caliphate, and those who were appointed as successors afterwards and ruled in their own time, one after another, followed them in that, the ruler carrying out an expedition himself every year, or sending someone out from his deputies on his behalf. It did not cease to be that way until the time in which one of the caliphs left off doing it because of his weakness. Others followed him in this for the reason mentioned, or a similar one. His stopping this, along with the necessary impositions on the Muslims which they threw off, and the forbidden things which they acted badly by doing, made it necessary that God dispersed their unity, split up their togetherness, threw enmity and hatred between them and tempted their enemies to snatch their country from their grasp.

A number of the enemy pounced on the island of Sicily while the Muslims disputed and competed, and they conquered in the same way one city after another in al-Andalus. When the reports confirmed for them that Syria suffered from the disagreement of its masters and its rulers' being unaware of its deficiencies and needs, they confirmed their resolution to set out for it, and Jerusalem was their dearest wish … They looked out over Syria, on separated kingdoms, disunited hearts and differing views linked with hidden resentment, and with that their desires became stronger and extended to everything they saw. They did not stop, tireless in fighting the jihad against the Muslims. The Muslims were sluggish, and were reluctant to engage in combat until the enemy conquered more than their greatest hopes had conceived of the country, and destroyed and humiliated many times the number of people that they had wished. Still now they are spreading further in their efforts, assiduous in seeking an increase in their profits. Their desires are multiplying all the time because of what appears to be the Muslims' abstinence from opposing them, and their hopes are invigorated by virtue of what they see of their enemies' contentedness with being unharmed by them, until they have become convinced that the whole country will become theirs and all its people will be prisoners in their hands. May God in his generosity humble their ideas by bringing together everyone and arranging the unity of the people, for he is near, and answers prayers.

■ How does al-Sulami explain the weakness of the Muslims?

What exactly does the extract reveal about al-Sulami's views on the motivation of the crusaders?

■ Make a source summary for al-Sulami's *Book of Holy War*.

Al-Sulami's words were powerful, but they had little effect. On one occasion only six people attended his sermon in the Great Mosque at Damascus! In the early years of the twelfth century, the concept of jihad remained alive among some religious scholars, but it had not yet been adopted by the divided leaders of the Muslim Near East. It was not until later in the 1140s that jihad was harnessed by Muslim's military leaders. Only then would they begin to drive out the Frankish settlers from Syria and Palestine.

William of Tyre's *Historia*

William of Tyre was born in Palestine around the year 1130. In 1165, after studying in Paris and Bologna, he returned to the Kingdom of Jerusalem becoming Archbishop of Tyre in 1175. In 1184 William of Tyre completed the first history of the Kingdom of Jerusalem. His *Historia* is invaluable to historians because it provides a relatively reliable and detailed account of the history of Outremer from the time of the First Crusade. William of Tyre's chronicle provides particularly useful insights into the formation of the **Military Orders**. These military-religious institutions, known as the **Knights Templar** and the **Knights of St John** (Hospitallers), played a crucial role in the formation and survival of the crusader states.

This photograph shows the place where the Knights Templar began – the **Haram al-Sharif** (Temple Mount) in Jerusalem. You can see the golden dome of the Dome of the Rock. On the far left is the smaller dome of the Aqsa Mosque. This was the main mosque of Jerusalem at the time of the First Crusade. In 1099 the crusaders converted the Dome of the Rock into a church which they called the 'Temple of the Lord'. They made the Aqsa Mosque a residence for Latin rulers of the Kingdom of Jerusalem. In 1119 a small band of knights offered to perform a service for the new king of Jerusalem, Baldwin II. They would police the road from Jaffa to Jerusalem in order to protect the Christian pilgrims visiting the Holy Land. In return, Baldwin II gave them part of the Aqsa Mosque for their headquarters. These soldier-monks became known as the Templars because of their proximity to the 'Temple of the Lord' on Haram al-Sharif. They were soon able to refurbish their headquarters at the Aqsa Mosque creating an impressive military barracks and arsenal.

The example set by the Templars was followed by the monks in the Hospital of St John in Jerusalem. The Hospitallers, as they were later known, became the second Military Order in the crusader states. Members of both orders took vows of poverty, chastity and obedience, but they also vowed to defend the Holy Land through the sword. Very quickly, the Templars and Hospitallers became enormously wealthy. They attracted widespread support from the nobles of Europe who showed their devotion to God by giving land and money to the Military Orders. This enabled the Templars and Hospitallers to play a vital role in protecting the crusader states from Muslim attack. From the 1140s, the nobles of the Latin East began to give control of castles to the Military Orders, often allowing them to develop semi-autonomous territories on the borders of the crusader states.

The Templars and Hospitallers may have been popular with the nobility of Europe and the Near East, but they attracted criticism from sections of the clergy. Some clerics were appalled at the idea of monks killing people. Others disliked the fact that the Templars and Hospitallers were answerable only to the Pope in Rome and were free from the authority of Church leaders such as the Latin **patriarch** in Jerusalem. One cleric who made known his objections to the Templars and Hospitallers was William of Tyre. Here is his description of the Knights Templar.

In this year [1118] certain noble men of knightly rank, religious men, devoted to God and fearing him, bound themselves to Christ's service in the hands of the Lord Patriarch. They promised to live in perpetuity as monks, without possessions, under vows of chastity and obedience. Since they had no fixed abode, the King gave them a dwelling house near the Lord's Temple. Their primary duty, one which was enjoined upon them by the Lord Patriarch and other bishops for the remission of sins was that of protecting the roads and routes against the attacks of robbers and brigands. This they did especially in order to safeguard pilgrims.

For nine years after their founding, the knights wore secular clothing ... In their ninth year there was held in France, at Troyes, a council. This council, by command of the Lord Pope Honorius and the Lord Stephen, Patriarch of Jerusalem, established a rule for the knights and assigned them a white habit. Although the knights had now been established for nine years, there were still only nine of them. From this time onward their numbers began to grow and their possessions began to multiply. Later, in Pope Eugenius' time, it is said that both the knights and their humbler servants, called sergeants, began to affix crosses made of red cloth to their mantles so as to distinguish themselves from others. They have now grown so great that there are in this Order today about 300 knights who wear white mantles in addition to the brothers who are almost countless.

They are said to have immense possessions both here and overseas, so that there is now not a province in the Christian world which has not bestowed upon the aforesaid brothers a portion of its goods. It is said that their wealth is equal to the treasures of kings. Because they have their headquarters in the royal palace next to the Temple of the Lord they are called the Brothers of the Militia of the Temple. Although they maintained their establishment honourably for a long time and fulfilled their vocation with sufficient prudence, later, because of the neglect of humility, they withdrew from the Patriarch of Jerusalem, by whom their order was founded and from whom they received their first benefices and to whom they denied the obedience which their predecessors rendered. They have also taken away tithes and first fruits from God's churches, have disturbed their possessions, and have made themselves exceedingly troublesome.

■ What does this extract from William of Tyre's *Historia* reveal about his attitude towards the Knights Templar?

In what ways were the Templars and Hospitallers important in the formation of the crusader states?

Make a source summary for William of Tyre's *Historia*.

Queen Melisende's Psalter

In August 1131, Baldwin II, King of Jerusalem, died. You can see Baldwin on his death bed in the top part of this thirteenth-century illustration from a French copy of William of Tyre's *Historia*. The King had made careful plans for the succession following his death. Baldwin II had four daughters with his Armenian wife, Morphia, but no sons. The King's priority was therefore a good match for his eldest daughter, Melisende. In 1129, after long negotiations, Melisende married Fulk, Count of Anjou, one of the most powerful noblemen in France. Fulk must have been delighted at the prospect of becoming the most important ruler in the crusader states. However, from his deathbed, Baldwin II made a startling announcement. In order to ensure that his own dynasty would continue to rule the Kingdom of Jerusalem, he committed his state not to Fulk alone, but to the joint rule of Fulk, Melisende and their two-year-old son Baldwin. The bottom half of the illustration depicts the coronation of Fulk, but, on 14 September 1131, in the Church of the Holy Sepulchre, both Fulk *and* Melisende were crowned and anointed as joint rulers of the Kingdom of Jerusalem.

Fulk must have been furious at Baldwin's decision. He had not surrendered his powerful position as Count of Anjou in order to share power as King of Jerusalem with his wife! Following the coronation, Fulk largely ignored the requirement to rule jointly and deliberately sidelined the Queen. He also started to give land and power in the Kingdom of Jerusalem to his own Angevin followers. Within three years of the coronation, Fulk's unwillingness to rule jointly with his wife and Melisende's determination to uphold her power to the full, led to troubles in their marriage and brought the Kingdom of Jerusalem to the brink of civil war. The champion of Melisende's cause was Hugh, the 28-year-old Count of Jaffa of whom William of Tyre wrote: '… in respect of physical beauty and nobility of birth, as well as experience in the art of war, he hath no equal in the kingdom'. As one of the most important nobles in the Kingdom of Jerusalem, Hugh of Jaffa was determined that King Fulk should not be allowed to weaken the power of the native nobility. He was also determined to preserve the bloodline of Melisende. During the early 1130s tensions grew between Fulk and Hugh of Jaffa. Rumours of a sexual relationship between Melisende and Hugh made matters worse.

In 1134, Hugh and his associates were accused of plotting to murder King Fulk. They were found guilty of high treason and sentenced to three years in exile. The lenient punishment given to Hugh of Jaffa must surely have been due to Melisende's influence on her husband. She may have persuaded Fulk that to sentence Hugh to execution would have humiliated her and risked a civil war in the Kingdom of Jerusalem. While Hugh of Jaffa waited for his exile to begin, he was attacked on the streets of Jerusalem by an unknown assassin who set upon him with a sword. Despite his serious injuries, Hugh survived. Some people suspected that Fulk lay behind the botched attempted murder. This tipped the balance

△ The death of Baldwin II and the coronation of Fulk, 1131. A miniature in William of Tyre, *Historia Rerum in Partibus Transmarinis Gestarum*, thirteenth century.

◼ Why do you think the artist might have shown only Fulk's coronation?

◼ What do the first four years of Queen Melisende's reign reveal about the strengths and weaknesses of the Kingdom of Jerusalem in the early 1130s?

△ A page from the Melisende Psalter showing Christ's entry into Jerusalem.

What does the Melisende Psalter reveal about the range of influences on art in the crusader states?

Make a source summary for Queen Melisende's Psalter.

of power in favour of Melisende. From 1135, Fulk seems to have begun to rule in partnership with his wife as Baldwin II had decreed.

A remarkable work of art suggests that Fulk tried to make amends with his wife in the years following Hugh of Jaffa's exile. The King commissioned an exquisite gift that he hoped might help to restore their marriage. Melisende was known for her piety and for her love of books, so Fulk gave her a beautifully-crafted psalter – a prayer book and religious guide. The Melisende Psalter, one of the rarest and most beautiful treasures to come from the crusader states, can still be seen in the British Library. It is quite small – about the size of a modern paperback – but what it lacks in size it makes up for in beauty.

Art historians think that at least seven people worked on the psalter. The covers were made from intricately carved ivory studded with turquoise, ruby and emerald stones. The front cover shows stories of King David from the Old Testament. The back cover, which you can see on page 63, depicts a monarch dressed in the style of a Byzantine ruler. This is probably meant to represent Fulk. The King carries out the acts of mercy as specified in the book of Matthew: giving out food and drink, helping the sick, visiting prisoners, clothing the poor, and sheltering strangers. Between the roundels you can see birds and animals and, around the edge, Islamic-style design. Inside, the Melisende Psalter contains 24 hand-coloured illuminations of scenes from the New Testament. The team of illustrators included a Byzantine-trained 'crusader' artist and a scribe from Northern France.

Some art historians have argued that the Melisende Psalter represents a distinctive 'crusader art' in which different influences were integrated to create a unique style during the twelfth century. They point to a similar mixture of influences that can also be found in the building work Queen Melisende commissioned during the 1140s. The architecture and decoration of the Queen's biggest building project – the re-design of the Church of the Holy Sepulchre – also contained a mixture of eastern and western styles when it was completed in 1149. Does the art and architecture of the Kingdom of Jerusalem reveal wider truths about the crusader states in the first part of the twelfth century? It certainly does not reflect an entirely brutal and intolerant regime intent on the destruction of Islam in the Near East. But nor does it suggest a 'melting pot' of cross-cultural connections and exchanges.

△ The back cover of the Melisende Psalter, made *c.* 1135.

The site of Castellum Regis

△ A photograph of Castellum Regis.

Historical research is not just about sitting in archives reading old documents. Sometimes historians get their boots muddy (or at least dusty) by studying historic sites. Our fifth source in this enquiry is a historic site at Mi'ilya in western Galilee, ten kilometres north-east of Acre. In the twelfth century the village was known as Castellum Regis. In the 1990s, Ronnie Ellenblum (Professor of Historical Geography at the Hebrew University of Jerusalem) studied not only the medieval documents relating to Castellum Regis, but also the archaeology of the site. He made some surprising discoveries. The remains of the crusader fortress in the centre of the village were well known, but careful analysis of land transactions in the written documents, combined with a detailed investigation of the site, revealed that Castellum Regis was much more than a fortress.

Castellum Regis was a carefully-planned and extensive rural settlement. The village was built on the slope of a hill and was surrounded by a wall eight to ten metres high. Inside the wall Ellenblum identified the remains of seventeen houses which had been occupied by Frankish settlers. Many of the modern houses were built on the foundations of crusaders' houses. One building still has the same use as in crusader times – an oil press. A house that is slightly larger than the rest contains a stone carved with a large cross inside a circle. The documents showed that the house belonged to the Bishop of Acre. Between the houses and the wall is an empty stretch of land that probably contained gardens in the eleventh century. At the top end of the village the Christian church stands on the foundations of the original crusaders' church. Outside the walls, documents and fieldwork revealed terraces of fields and vineyards laid out by the Frankish settlers. A network of roads, some of which were built by the Franks, connected Castellum Regis to neighbouring villages. The only building outside the walls – a leper house – was a grim reminder of the prevalence of leprosy on the Middle Ages.

The investigation of Castellum Regis revealed that it was a totally new settlement created by the Franks in the early twelfth century. The settlers did not take over an existing Byzantine village, but chose to build a new settlement on a nearby hill. The evidence from this single village seemed to fit neither to the 'assimilation' nor the 'segregation' model of society in the crusader states. The Franks lived separately in their own village, but were clearly prepared to settle in rural areas. It would seem that they did not entirely confine themselves to towns and fortresses for fear of Muslim attack.

■ Begin your source summary for the site of Castellum Regis.

The overall pattern of settlement

The study of an individual settlement like Castellum Regis can be very revealing, but it leaves questions about the overall pattern of Frankish settlement unanswered. Detailed documents such as those relating to the land and buildings of Castellum Regis are rare, but manuscripts often contain indirect references to crusader settlements. In order to find out about the overall pattern of settlement, Ellenblum re-examined documents used by previous generations of historians and combined this documentary research with field study of more than 200 Frankish settlements in the Kingdom of Jerusalem. In the process he discovered some previously unknown sites and made some startling discoveries about the nature and pattern of Frankish settlement.

It appears that the Franks were not just fighters and builders of fortifications, but were also very successful settlers. The migrants who began to farm in the Kingdom of Jerusalem built an extensive network of rural settlements. They constructed unfortified villages, manor houses, farm houses, flour mills, monasteries and churches. The settlers established new fields and vineyards, and learned how to cultivate crops such as sugar cane. To link their settlements the Franks built a network of new roads and bridges. At the beginning of the twelfth century the priority of the crusaders was military conquest, but from the 1120s it seems that Frankish settlers wanted to farm, build houses, and raise families rather than risk death in the name of God. From 1120 until 1160 the Kingdom of Jerusalem was mostly peaceful and this enabled the Franks to focus on farming and trading.

Ellenblum's map demonstrates that the Franks settled much more extensively than historians had previously thought, but it also reveals a particular pattern to Frankish settlement. When the crusaders arrived in Palestine in 1099 the land was divided between the local Muslim and the Christian populations. The Franks refrained almost completely from settling in purely Muslim areas. Instead, they established their settlements in territories already settled by local Christians. The Franks who settled in Outremer had close relations with eastern Christians, but kept apart from the Muslim population who lived elsewhere in the Kingdom of Jerusalem. It would seem, therefore, that neither the French model of 'assimilation' nor the post-colonial model of 'segregation' is sufficient to explain the complex reality of settlement in the crusader states.

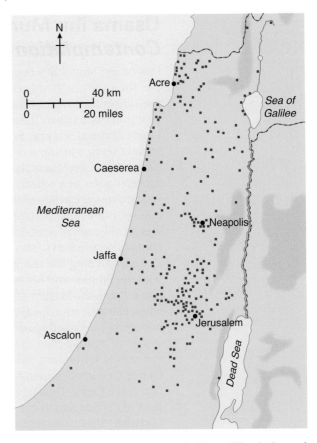

△ Map of Frankish rural sites in the Kingdom of Jerusalem.

■ Complete your source summary for the site of Castellum Regis.

In the third section of your source summary make sure you summarise what the overall pattern of settlement reveals about the nature of crusader society.

Usama ibn Munqidh's *Book of Contemplation*

Usama ibn Munqidh's *Book of Contemplation* is a rare Muslim source that can shed some light on relations between Franks and Muslims in the twelfth century. Usama was born into a Syrian noble family in 1095, the year that Pope Urban II summoned the First Crusade. In 1131 he left the family home at Shayzar in northern Syria and began a career that would include service to some of the most important rulers of the Muslim Near East. Usama ibn Munqidh was a skilled warrior and diplomat, but it was his reputation as a scholar and poet that Muslim rulers most admired. It was at around the age of 90, following his final post at the court of Saladin, that Usama wrote his *Kitab al-I'tibar*, (*Book of Contemplation*). The book was a collection of anecdotes from his own life intended to show how God controls people's destinies.

Usama's long life and varied career meant that he had much contact with the Franks, and his *Book of Contemplation* contains several anecdotes about Frankish–Muslim encounters. However, we have to be careful when using Usama ibn Munqidh's writing as evidence of the relationship between Franks and Muslims. Usama aimed to entertain his readers as well as to instruct them. He often wrote about unusual events and his comments sometimes reflect a stereotypical Muslim view of the Franks. Usama frequently ended his accounts of the Franks with the words 'May God curse them!' However, if used with caution, Usama ibn Munqidh's *Book of Contemplation* can provide fascinating glimpses into the nature of Christian–Muslim relations.

One of the most surprising revelations from the *Book of Contemplation* is the way in which Usama ibn Munqidh related to the Franks in an amicable and courteous way. In one particular extract Usama described his friendship with a Frankish knight:

■ What does this extract reveal about the relationship between Usama ibn Munqidh and the Christian knight?

How does each man show that he thinks he is culturally superior to the other?

In the army of King Fulk, son of Fulk, there was a respected Frankish knight who had come from their country just to go on pilgrimage and then return home. He grew to like my company and he became my constant companion, calling me 'my brother'. Between us there were ties of amity and sociability. When he resolved to take the sea back to his country, he said to me: 'My brother, I am leaving for my country. I want you to send your son (my son, who was with me was fourteen years old) with me to my country, where he can observe the knights and observe reason and **chivalry**. When he returns, he will be like a truly rational man'. And so there fell upon my ears words that would never come from a truly rational head!

Parts of Usama ibn Munqidh's *Book of Contemplation* can help us to appreciate the complex religious attitudes in eleventh-century Outremer. During the first ten years of the crusader states, we have seen that Muslims in towns who resisted conquest could be brutally murdered. The crusaders also introduced harsh laws to ensure the separation of Muslims and Christians. For example, the decrees of Nablus (1120) enacted that sexual intercourse between Christians and Muslims was to be punished by castration for men while women were to have their noses cut off. As well as introducing legal restrictions like the decrees of Nablus on Muslims, the Franks also converted some mosques into churches. However, there is little evidence of the forced conversion of Muslims and, across the crusader states, many mosques continued to function. In the early 1140s Usama ibn Munqidh was able to visit the Aqsa Mosque in Jerusalem. In a revealing account from his *Book of Contemplation* Usama contrasts the behaviour of the Templars with that of the newly-arrived Franks:

Anyone who is recently arrived from the Frankish lands is rougher in character than those who have become acclimated and have frequented the company of Muslims. Here is an instance of their rough character (may God abominate them!):

Whenever I went to visit the holy sites in Jerusalem, I would go in and make my way up to the Aqsa Mosque, beside which stood a small mosque that the Franks had converted into a church. When I went into the Aqsa Mosque – where the Templars who are my friends, were – they would clear out that little mosque so that I could pray in it. One day, I went into the little mosque, recited the opening formula 'God is great!' and stood up in prayer. At this one of the Franks rushed at me and grabbed me and turned my face towards the east, saying, 'Pray like *this*!' A group of Templars hurried towards him, took hold of the Frank and took him away from me. I then returned to my prayers. The Frank, that very same one, took advantage of their inattention and returned, rushing upon me and turning my face to the east, saying, 'Pray like *this*!' So the Templars came in again, grabbed him and threw him out. They apologised to me, saying, 'This man is a stranger just arrived from the Frankish lands sometime in the past few days. He has never before seen anyone who did not pray towards the east.' 'I think I've prayed quite enough,' I said and left. I used to marvel at that devil the change of his expression, the way he trembled and what he must have made of seeing someone praying towards Makkah.

▨ What does the incident reveal about the Franks' attitudes towards Usama ibn-Munqidh and towards the Muslim population in general?

What does Usama's account reveal about his attitudes towards the Franks?

Remember to complete your final source summary on Usama ibn-Munqidh's *Book of Contemplation*.

▨ Concluding your enquiry

Now use the information in your source summaries to:

1 explain how the crusader states were formed in the first decades of the twelfth century
2 describe the nature of the society that emerged in the crusader states.

Crusader castles: What were they really for?

This is the mighty Crac des Chevaliers, the most famous of all the crusader castles. Most of the castles now lie in ruins, but Crac stands mostly intact, dominating the valley between the Mediterranean coast and the inland town of Homs. In 1144, Raymond II, Count of Tripoli, gave the fortress and the surrounding lands to the Knights Hospitallers in order to defend the eastern frontier of his territory. Over the following decades, and particularly after 1202 when an earthquake damaged part of the fortress, the Hospitallers developed Crac des Chevaliers into the largest and most formidable castle in the crusader states. The annotated reconstruction on the opposite page helps you to understand what made Crac such an impressive fortress.

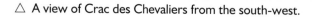

△ A view of Crac des Chevaliers from the south-west.

Water tank

An aqueduct from a neighbouring hill provided the castle with drinking water and a moat. Water was stored in a great outdoor water tank and in nine underground cisterns. This would enable the castle to withstand a siege for several months.

Small inner courtyard

A chapel, hall and massive vaults were built in three-quarters of the inner courtyard. The heavy stone vaults were built against the inner walls to provide store-rooms, stables and living quarters. In the early thirteenth century the castle could accommodate around 60 knights and 2000 infantrymen.

▷ An artist's reconstruction of Crac des Chevaliers as it was in the thirteenth century. This is the view from the north-east.

Covered entrance

A tunnel ran from the outer gate to the centre of the castle. Halfway along, the tunnel made a hairpin bend and doubled back to reach the entrance of the inner courtyard. The Hospitallers built murder-holes in the roof of the tunnel so that they could attack the enemy from above.

External wall and towers

The Hospitallers built a massive outer wall which transformed Crac into a concentric castle. At the base, the wall was four metres wide in order to prevent tunnelling. The knights constructed high round towers, projecting from the walls. The towers had arrow slits at different levels and upper platforms which could support catapults.

Postern gate

This was built into the outside wall of the castle. It allowed troops to leave the castle in order to fight the enemy outside the walls.

Crac des Chevaliers is the most iconic of all the crusader castles, but we should not let Crac dominate our view of what these castles were really for. Until recently, historians assumed that crusader castles were necessary because the Frankish settlers faced almost constant danger of Muslim attack. They argued that the Franks were vastly outnumbered and that it was therefore necessary to protect the territory of the crusader states by building formidable fortresses. This interpretation reinforced the 'segregationist' view of crusader society which depicted the Franks as a minority group imposing military rule on the local population. However, in recent years, pioneering research, summarised on the next two pages, has given us a better and more complex understanding of what crusader castles were really for.

Crusader castles: What were they really for?

In 2007, Ronnie Ellenblum wrote a book which transformed our understanding of crusader castles. *Crusader Castles and Modern Histories* was based on years of painstaking research in archives and at archaeological sites. What made Ellenblum's work particularly groundbreaking was his willingness to ask new and interesting questions about crusader castles:

- Did the borders that castles were meant to defend really exist in the twelfth and thirteenth centuries?

- What can we discover about the smaller structures that are far more typical of crusader castles than huge fortresses like Crac des Chevaliers?

- How exactly did the building of castles relate to the changing relationship between the Franks and the Muslims?

Ellenblum argued that fixed and geographically divided borders were a product of nineteenth-century nation states and that the idea of a defined border could not be applied to the Middle Ages. It was a mistake, therefore, to think that castles were constructed to defend a fixed frontier in the territory occupied by the Franks. Ellenblum's systematic research allowed him to locate and date 165 fortified sites. This led him to suggest three phases of crusader castle building during the twelfth century.

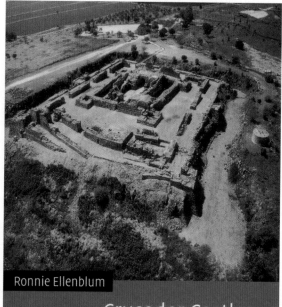

Ronnie Ellenblum

Crusader Castles and Modern Histories

CAMBRIDGE

△ Ellenblum's book on crusader castles built on his earlier study of settlement in the Kingdom of Jerusalem.

First generation crusader castles (1099–1115)

During the first fifteen years of their reign, at least 25 castles were conquered or newly-built by the crusaders (indicated in red on the map opposite).Twenty-one sites had been in existence before the arrival of the Franks and continued after the conquest. Eight fortifications were completely new. It seems that, in the first phase of construction, the Franks tended to build fortifications mainly in the cities and villages which they took from the Muslims, but that they also created some new rural and urban settlements.

Second generation crusader castles (1115–69)

The years between 1115 and 1169 were a period of calm in crusading history when the Kingdom of Jerusalem was relatively secure. Yet this was a period of intensive castle building. These were mainly new fortifications built in rural and remote areas (indicated in blue on the map). Many of these castles were small and simple structures enclosed by a single wall. Ellenblum found little correlation between the location of second generation castles and areas of military confrontation. He concluded that most of these castles were built as centres of administration and agricultural production, not as defence against external attack. It was the flourishing rural economy of the Frankish territory which led to the construction of so many castles in these years.

Third generation crusader castles (1168–87)

In the early 1160s the balance of power between the crusader states and the Muslims began to change. By the middle of the decade the Muslims had succeeded in taking some important Frankish cities and castles. The castles which the Franks built or renovated in the twenty years after 1168 (indicated in orange on the map) were located in the regions under threat in the east, north-east and south-west of the kingdom. These third generation castles tended to be larger and better fortified than earlier crusader castles.

Ronnie Ellenblum's research has given us a more complex understanding of the nature and purpose of crusader castles. He has demonstrated that, during the first 70 years of the Latin Kingdom of Jerusalem, castles were often built for economic and geographical rather than strategic reasons. Very few were built in areas under danger of attack. Only from the late 1160s did the Franks begin to build large concentric castles capable of withstanding long sieges. Ellenblum's work has shown that, if we are to understand what crusader castles were really for, we need to see them in the context of the changing balance of power between Franks and the Muslims in the Near East.

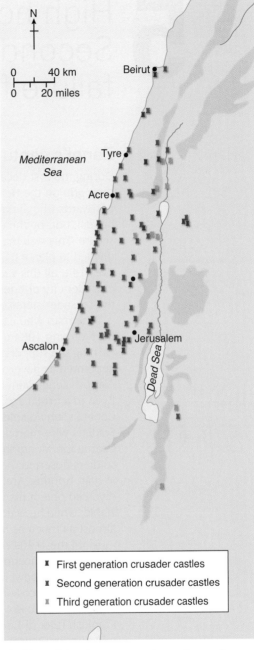

✕ First generation crusader castles

✕ Second generation crusader castles

✕ Third generation crusader castles

△ Map of the three generations of crusader castles identified by Ronnie Ellenblum.

5 High hopes: Why did the Second Crusade end in failure for the Christians?

Zengi's capture of Edessa, December 1144

During the first decades of the twelfth century, the Franks tightened their grip on the Near East. True, the Franks did not manage to expand eastwards (the Syrian cities of Aleppo and Damascus remained in Muslim hands), but, by the early 1140s, the four crusader states seemed relatively secure. This was mainly because the Muslims of the Near East were too divided to plan a co-ordinated attack on the Franks. Then, on Christmas Eve 1144, all this suddenly changed when Muslim forces captured the crusader city of Edessa. This was the first major setback in the history of the crusader states.

The man who captured Edessa for the Muslims was Imad ad-Din Zengi. Born around 1084 to a Turkish warlord, Zengi rose to power in the 1120s, earning the support of the Seljuk sultan of Baghdad. By 1127 he had been appointed as governor of Mosul. The following year, he seized control of Aleppo. Zengi gained a reputation as a ruthless and fearsome warrior. Even in a brutal age, his capacity for violence and cruelty was legendary. Generals who displeased him were exiled, and their sons were castrated. Soldiers who marched out of line and trampled on crops were crucified. Usama ibn Munqidh, who served Zengi's court, wrote that if one of Zengi's soldiers deserted, he would order the two neighbouring men to be cut in half. Another Arab chronicler described how Zengi, in a drunken fury, divorced one of his wives and had her gang-raped by the grooms in his stable, while he watched. Zengi must have been feared by his followers almost as much as by his enemies.

Until the 1140s Zengi showed little interest in attacking the Franks. Instead, he concentrated on advancing into southern Syria and on extending his power base in Iraq. From 1143, Zengi focused on fighting the minor princes of northern Iraq. He only attacked the crusader city of Edessa because of a pact between one of these Iraqi warlords and the Frankish ruler of Edessa, Joscelin II. In the autumn of 1144 Zengi's spies told him that Joscelin II had left Edessa and that few troops remained in the city. Zengi acted swiftly. His troops reached Edessa in late November and began a devastating attack on the city's great walls using siege towers and tunnels. On Christmas eve, Zengi inspected the tunnels and gave the order to set fire to the wooden props and beams that supported them. Within a short time, a section of Edessa's wall collapsed. Zengi's men flooded into the city. The terrified Christians fled towards the citadel. Hundreds were crushed to death in the panic. Those who reached the fortress held out for two more days, but, by 26 December, the whole of Edessa was in Muslim hands. Zengi ordered that the native Christians should be spared, but he slaughtered the Frankish men, enslaved their women and destroyed their churches.

Zengi's capture of Edessa filled the Franks of the Near East with fear. They were horrified at the prospect of a domino effect in which, one by one, the crusader states fell to Zengi's forces. The Frankish chronicler William of Tyre described 1144 as an 'ominous disaster' and observed that there was now a real danger of the Muslims 'overrunning the entire east unchecked'. It was this fear that prompted an appeal to western Europe for help. The response was one of the largest military expeditions of the Middle Ages – the Second Crusade.

■ An overview of the Second Crusade

You can begin to get to grips with the Second Crusade by looking carefully at the map below and the table of key events on the next page. Use the map and table of key events to answer the following questions:

- Who were the leaders of the Crusade?

- Which routes did the crusaders take to the Near East?
- How long did the Second Crusade last?
- Which particular places were important in the Crusade?
- Did the crusaders recapture Edessa?

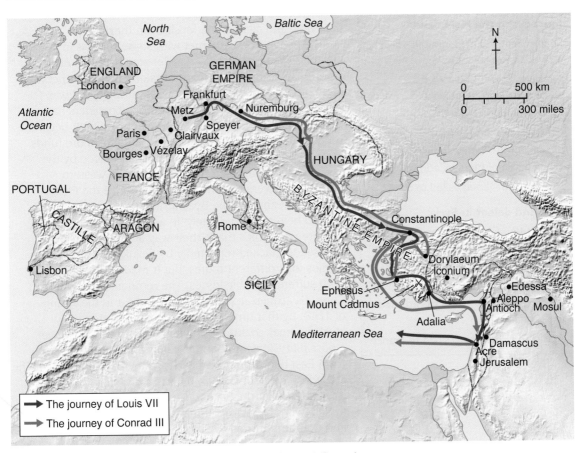

△ The journeys of Louis VII and Conrad III on the Second Crusade.

Key events of the Second Crusade

26 December 1144 Zengi, ruler of Mosul and Aleppo, captured the city of Edessa

Preaching and preparing

1 December 1145 Pope Eugenius III issued the Papal bull *Quantum praedecessores*

Easter 1146 Bernard of Clairvaux preached at Vézelay accompanied by Louis VII, King of France

Christmas 1146 Bernard of Clairvaux preached at Speyer. Conrad, King of Germany, took the cross

May 1147 Conrad III departed from Nuremburg

June 1147 Louis VII departed from Metz

Journeys to the Holy Land

September 1147 Conrad III's army arrived in Constantinople

October 1147 Louis VII's army arrived in Constantinople

October 1147 Conrad's forces defeated near Dorylaeum

January 1148 Louis' forces defeated at the battle of Mount Cadmus

March 1148 Louis sailed to Syria

War and defeat in Syria

June 1148 Conference at Acre agreed to attack Damascus

July 1148 Crusaders defeated at Damascus

September 1148 Conrad returned to Germany

April 1149 Louis returned to France

The Second Crusade began with high hopes. The Crusade was launched on 1 December 1145 when Pope Eugenius III issued the bull *Quantum praedecessores*. The **papal bull** was crucial, the centrepiece of the Church's recruitment drive. It clearly argued the need for a new crusade and set out the privileges that people could expect if they took part. In the spring and summer of 1146 huge numbers of people responded to the Pope's call for Holy War. Many more people joined the Crusade on hearing the eloquent and dynamic preaching of the Cistercian abbot, Bernard of Clairvaux. Bernard's well-organised preaching tour was an important factor in the remarkable response to the call for a crusade. Recruitment was also boosted by the leadership of the two greatest kings of western Europe: Conrad III of Germany and Louis VII of France. This was the first time that major European monarchs risked leaving their kingdoms to make the dangerous journey to the Holy Land. But the Holy Land was not the only focus of the Second Crusade. This was a Holy War on three fronts. While the kings of France and Germany led their vast armies to the Near East, other forces fought against the pagan tribes of the Baltic and against the Muslims in **Iberia**.

The Second Crusade met with some success in Iberia, but the expedition to the crusader states was an utter failure. The crippling expense of taking huge numbers of knights and non-combatants to the Holy Land was a problem from the outset. The French crusaders had reached no further than Hungary when Louis VII began sending urgent messages to Paris asking for more funds. Lack of money was not the only problem faced by the crusaders. The troubled relations between western European powers and the Byzantines since the First Crusade meant that the Byzantine emperor, Manuel I, offered help only grudgingly. In addition, as the German and French armies made their way across Anatolia, they were attacked repeatedly by Seljuk Turk forces. The armies took different routes, but it made little difference. Both suffered terrible losses. The remnants of Louis' and Conrad's armies arrived in the Latin East in the spring of 1148. By that time Edessa had been destroyed by Muslim forces so attempting its recovery was no longer a possibility. Instead, Conrad, Louis and the rulers of the Latin East decided on Damascus as a viable alternative. The crusaders' siege of Damascus was a disaster. In July 1148, it was clear that the Second Crusade had failed miserably to deal with the Islamic threat to the crusader states. Louis and Conrad returned to Europe angry and humiliated.

■ **Enquiry Focus:** Why did the Second Crusade end in failure for the Christians?

From what you have discovered so far, you may already have some initial ideas about why the Second Crusade failed. Your challenge in this enquiry is to construct a clear, well-structured and detailed explanation of why, in your view, the Second Crusade ended in failure for the Christians. We have organised the narrative around the three main phases of the Second Crusade:

1 **Preaching and preparing**, December 1145 to May 1147
2 **Journeys to the Holy Land**, May 1147 to March 1148
3 **War and defeat in Syria**, March 1148 to July 1148

As you read about each of these phases you should collect ideas and information in the different 'factor folders' that you can see below. You may find that the same event or issue can be included in more than one folder. At the end of the enquiry you will be able to use the ideas and information in your 'factor folders' to explain why, in your opinion, the Second Crusade ended in failure for the Christians.

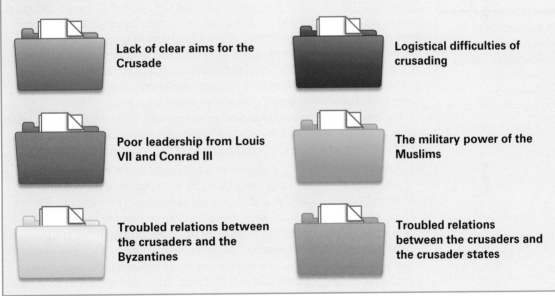

Lack of clear aims for the Crusade

Logistical difficulties of crusading

Poor leadership from Louis VII and Conrad III

The military power of the Muslims

Troubled relations between the crusaders and the Byzantines

Troubled relations between the crusaders and the crusader states

Preaching and preparing, December 1145 to May 1147

Eugenius III and *Quantum praedecessores*

From a twenty-first century perspective, it seems like a long time between the capture of Edessa by Zengi on Christmas Eve 1144 and the launch of the Second Crusade on 1 December 1145. But, in the twelfth century, news travelled by horses and boats rather than by the internet. The papal court in Italy may not have heard of the disaster until May 1145. It was not until November 1145 that envoys from Antioch and Jerusalem arrived in Italy with an official request for help addressed to the new Pope, Eugenius III. However, simply because *Quantum praedecessores* was not issued until 1 December 1145, does not mean that the papacy hadn't already given some thought to the situation in the crusader states. In fact, an analysis of the papal bull shows that it was a carefully-researched and skilfully-written document that provided a powerful case for the Second Crusade. *Quantum praedecessores* challenged people to take the cross by emphasising some important themes: the suffering of the Christians in the East; the need to live up to the achievements of the First Crusade; and the divine authority of Eugenius III. The bull offered potential crusaders remission of all sins, protection for their families and property while they were away and exemption from payment of interest on loans and debts.

The power of *Quantum praedecessores* was one reason why such a wide range of people were inspired to take the cross. However, the papal bull had two flaws which weakened the Second Crusade from the outset:

1   Enlisting the right type of person was crucial to the success of the Crusade. This was a dilemma faced by the crusading movement throughout the twelfth and thirteenth centuries. The most crucial people on any crusade were those capable of fighting, but crusades were pilgrimages that were open to all. Non-combatant recruits – monks, peasants, craftsmen, paupers, women and children – swelled the number of crusaders, but these people needed food, water and shelter on the journey to the Holy Land. They also required protection from attack. Ensuring a balance between fighters and non-fighters was crucial. *Quantum praedecessores* made a half-hearted attempt to get to grips with this issue by stating that 'those who are on God's side and especially the more powerful and the nobles' should join the Crusade, but the problem of balancing an effective fighting force with mass appeal remained unresolved. As we shall see, the large number of non-combatants who joined the Second Crusade would endure terrible suffering and hardship during the campaign.

2   *Quantum praedecessores* was also problematic because Eugenius' text was unclear about the exact goal of the Second Crusade. As we should expect, the document mentioned the fate of Edessa, but it did not state explicitly that the city should be recaptured. Nor did it name Zengi as an enemy of the crusader states. Instead, *Quantum praedecessores* vaguely challenged the crusaders to defend Jerusalem and to imitate the deeds of the first crusaders. This lack of clarity about the target of the Crusade opened the door for disputes between the Crusade's leaders and the rulers of the crusader states about the direction and focus of the Second Crusade.

> Papal bulls were known by their opening words. *Quantum praedecessores* means 'How greatly our predecessors ...'

> ■ Start to add ideas and information to some of your factor folders. Points from the first flaw can be included in the 'Logistical difficulties of crusading' folder. Points from the second flaw can be used to start your 'Lack of clear aims for the Crusade' folder.

Louis VII

Eugenius III may have issued *Quantum praedecessores* at the beginning of December 1145 because he thought that the French king Louis VII would be receptive to the idea of a crusade. In the early years of his reign, the King was keen to assert his authority, and some of his actions suggest that he could be impulsive. He became embroiled in heated disputes with the papacy and in a bitter feud with the Count of Champagne. In 1143, at the height of this conflict, Louis' troops burned down a church in Vitry allegedly containing hundreds of people. The King seems to have deeply regretted this atrocity later. In 1144–45, as tensions with the papacy and the Count of Champagne eased, there is evidence that Louis may have been considering a pilgrimage to Jerusalem. In the autumn of 1145, when envoys from Antioch and Jerusalem brought news of the capture of Edessa, they found the French king receptive to their request for help.

The King's Christmas court in 1145 was held in Bourges. It is unlikely that *Quantum praedecessores* reached Louis VII before Christmas, but the King had already made up his mind to lead a crusade. Louis invited his bishops and nobles to his Christmas court in larger numbers than usual and presented them with his plan to aid the Christians in the crusader states. The response was lukewarm, but it was agreed that the issue should be considered again the following Easter after discussions with Abbot Bernard of Clairvaux, the leading figure in the twelfth-century western Church. Bernard first preached the Second Crusade during the Easter week assembly at the Vézelay in Northern Burgundy. The Pope had re-issued *Quantum praedecessores* on 1 March and, with Louis VII, had planned a huge recruitment drive at Vézelay. So many people turned up that the abbey church was too small to accommodate them. On Easter Sunday, Bernard and Louis delivered rousing speeches from a hastily-constructed wooden platform in the field next to the abbey church. One observer noted that when Bernard had finished preaching, the call for crosses was so overwhelming that the bundle of cloth crosses that Bernard had brought soon ran out. The abbot tore up his own clothes to make more crosses. The clamour was so great that the wooden platform collapsed.

> ■ From what you have read about Louis VII, do you think there is anything about him that suggests he would be a problematic leader of the Second Crusade?

△ Bernard of Clairvaux preaching. It was Bernard of Clairvaux who, more than anyone else, created widespread support for the Crusade. In 1145 Bernard was in his 50s and at the height of his reputation as a brilliant preacher and writer. Before becoming pope, Eugenius III had been one of Bernard's monks. It is not surprising, therefore, that Eugenius turned to Bernard to popularise the message contained in *Quantum praedecessores*.

A thirteenth-century portrait of Conrad III. Conrad was the most powerful ruler in the Latin West. Aged around 50, the king was an experienced and pious ruler.

■ Add ideas and information to your factor folder on 'Poor leadership from Louis VII and Conrad III'.

Conrad III

Vézelay had been a huge success, but Bernard knew that the call for crusade had to reach an even wider audience. In the following months he therefore recruited a team of preachers to spread the word in other parts of France. He also sent letters to different parts of Europe including England, Northern Italy and Brittany. In the autumn of 1146, Bernard set out on a gruelling seven-month tour to preach in north-eastern France, Flanders and Germany. In November 1146, he reached Frankfurt where Conrad III, king of Germany, was holding his court. Conrad had already visited the Holy Land in 1124. He was also an important ally of the Pope against Norman Sicilian aggression in Italy.

The Second Crusade presented Conrad with an opportunity to further demonstrate his piety and to increase his prestige. However, at first, Conrad rejected Bernard's request that he should lead the Crusade. In 1146 Conrad was embroiled in conflicts both with the German nobility and with the King of Hungary; he was therefore reluctant to take the cross, fearful that his rivals may seize power. It was not until Bernard persuaded Conrad's main rival, Welf VI of Bavaria, to take the cross that Conrad felt that he could lead the Crusade. On 24 December 1146, Bernard joined Conrad for his Christmas court at Speyer. Four days later, following a dramatic sermon in which Bernard made a direct appeal to the King, Conrad took the cross. Louis VII and Conrad III – the two most powerful rulers in western Europe – were now leading the Crusade. But were the seeds of the Second Crusade's failure already sown? Conrad's army, like that of Louis', included family and friends, but also foes. Moreover, the fact that two strong monarchs were now leading the Crusade created the possibility of rivalry and tension in the months ahead.

Final preparations

During the early part of 1147, the Second Crusade not only broadened its participants, but also its targets. The Crusade had begun with the aim of aiding the Franks of the Near East, but it now widened to two other conflict zones in Iberia and the Baltic. Pope Eugenius gave support to King Alfonso VII of Castile in his attempt to take the southern Spanish city of Almeria from the Muslims. Bernard, too, encouraged crusaders to assist campaigns in Iberia, particularly a bid to retake the city of Lisbon. Then, in March 1147, as Bernard's preaching tour was drawing to a close, he was approached by some German crusaders who put forward a radical idea. Instead of crusading in the Holy Land, they wanted to attack the pagan tribes known as Wends who lived on the Baltic coast. Bernard and Eugenius supported the plan. Historians disagree about whether this widening of scope was directed and planned by the Crusade's leaders or whether it was a response to circumstances as they arose. It is clear, however, that the plan to recover Edessa was now only one part of an attack on the enemies of Christ in three different parts of Christendom. The aims of the Second Crusade had widened and the chances of success in the crusader states may have weakened.

As Louis and Conrad prepared for the campaign to the Holy Land in the spring of 1147, they faced some crucial decisions. Both monarchs would be leaving their realms for several months, possibly years, and they therefore had to give careful thought as to who should rule in their absence. Louis chose his childhood tutor, Abbot Suger of St Denis, to act as **regent**. In Germany, Conrad designated his ten-year-old son, Henry, as heir and chose a leading churchman, Abbot Wibald of Corvey as regent. The two monarchs were also preoccupied with the question of how to pay for such a huge crusade. As kings, both Conrad and Louis had access to large funds; however, in the early 1140s there had been a run of bad harvests in western Europe which meant that it was difficult for the monarchs to impose general taxes on their subjects. Instead, Conrad and Louis decided to levy money from towns and churches. This was only partially successful. Very soon after setting out for the Holy Land, Louis would be forced to write to Abbot Suger in Paris asking for more cash to buy food for the crusaders.

In the months before their departure, Conrad and Louis showed reassuring signs of co-operation. Representatives from their courts met to ensure the Crusade was properly co-ordinated. But the success of the Second Crusade would be dependent on more that the co-operation of the two kings. An underlying problem from the outset was the wider diplomatic situation in which the Crusade was launched. Both the Byzantine Emperor, Manuel I, and the Norman king of Sicily, Roger II, could provide crucial logistical support for the French and German Kings as they travelled to the crusader states, but the diplomatic situation in the 1140s meant that this was unlikely to happen:

- King Roger II of Sicily, was trying to expand his Norman kingdom in southern Italy and this brought him into conflict with both the papacy and the Byzantine Emperor, Manuel I. He was unlikely to provide support for the German King who was a natural ally of the papacy and Manuel I.

- Manuel I, the Byzantine Emperor, was suspicious of the French King because he had good relations with Roger II. In the spring of 1147, Manuel sent envoys to Louis and seemed willing to collaborate, but his underlying distrust of the French would undermine the Second Crusade in the months that followed.

Add these issues to your factor file on 'Troubled relations between the crusaders and the Byzantines'.

It was these wider diplomatic considerations that led to debate about which route should be taken to the Holy Land. Conrad only ever considered the overland route via the River Danube, the Balkans and Anatolia. The French, however, were divided as to whether to accept Roger II's offer to carry French troops by sea from the ports of southern Italy or to take the overland route. In the end, after much debate Louis decided on the overland route to the Near East. His departure was set for 15 June, a month later than Conrad's army was due to leave Germany. Louis' decision to take the overland route to the Holy Land via Constantinople and across Asia Minor would have terrible consequences.

See the map on page 73 to remind yourself of the places mentioned here.

■ Add ideas and information to your factor folders.

Which factors do you think might become particularly important in explaining the failure of the Second Crusade?

What was perhaps most surprising as the two kings made their final preparations for the Crusade is that there was no consultation with the Latin rulers of the crusader states. This may have been because Conrad and Louis expected to march directly across Anatolia to Edessa, but it could also have been due to the arrogance of the European kings. Why should such major kings be directed by the relatively minor rulers of the crusader states? That the French and German monarchs would pursue their own independent agendas in the Holy Land was a possibility from the very beginning of the Second Crusade.

Journeys to the Holy Land, May 1147 to March 1148

The main armies of the Second Crusade set off for the Near East in the early summer of 1147. The plan was to meet in Constantinople before heading on to Edessa. Conrad's forces departed in May 1147, followed by the French contingent in June. This staggered start was planned to allow both armies to follow the same route to Constantinople without exhausting local food supplies. In Constantinople, the Byzantine Emperor, Manuel I, must have viewed the Second Crusade as a worrying threat for the following reasons:

- If the Crusade succeeded, it would increase the power of the crusader states in northern Syria and this would challenge the recent resurgence of Byzantine authority in the region.

- Manuel was on good terms with the German King, but Conrad's absence from western Europe made an attack on Byzantine territory from Roger II more likely.

- Manuel I was afraid that elements of the French crusading army might join Roger II and attack the Byzantine Empire.

As the crusading armies approached Constantinople, Manuel decided to secure his eastern border by agreeing a temporary truce with the Seljuk Turks. Some of the crusaders saw this as an act of treachery.

Conrad III's journey to Constantinople and into Asia Minor

There were over 30,000 people in the crusading army that left Germany in May 1147. Conrad had hoped that his crusade would be mainly a professional force of trained soldiers, but this was not to be. Thousands of peasants joined. With such large numbers of non-combatants, the crusaders made slow progress, averaging only ten miles a day. The Germans made their way through Hungary without much trouble, but when they reached Byzantine territory Conrad's control began to slip. Manuel had ordered local markets to sell food to the crusaders, but this was often insufficient to feed such a large number of people. The crusaders began to plunder and skirmishes broke out. A drunken dispute with a Greek snake-charmer turned into a riot. People were killed. The Byzantine Emperor became increasingly anxious. By 7 September, the German army was just three days from Constantinople. Conrad set up camp on a flood plain, but disaster struck. A flash flood engulfed the German camp.

Crusaders and horses were drowned, and vital equipment was washed away. Conrad's bedraggled army reached Constantinople on 10 September. Manuel, fearful of a German attack, closed the gates of the city and stationed his troops along the walls.

The German forces camped outside the city walls while Conrad and Manuel exchanged frosty letters. Manuel was anxious for the Germans to move on into Asia Minor as quickly as possible and therefore supplied shipping to transport Conrad's army across the Bosphorus. He also provided guides to help the crusaders on their journey to the Holy land. Once in Asia Minor, instead of waiting for Louis as agreed, Conrad made the decision to press on. This was the point at which communications between the two royal leaders of the Crusade broke down. From Nicaea, Conrad chose to take the most direct route across Anatolia, heading for Dorylaeum and Iconium and then on to Antioch. This was the route that the First Crusaders had taken 50 years before. To allow his soldiers to move more quickly, Conrad placed his half-brother, Otto of Freising, in charge of the non-combatant pilgrims and ordered him to lead them along the safer coastal route.

The German crusaders and their Byzantine guides left Nicaea on 25 October. They carried as many supplies as possible, but, after ten days, and with another ten to go before reaching Iconium, their food began to run out. As the crusaders approached the area around Dorylaeum they found themselves in an infertile and largely uninhabitable environment where food and water were scarce. The territory was also dangerous because it was close to the border with the Seljuk Turks. As Conrad's forces foraged for food, they came under constant attack from the lightning cavalry raids of the Turkish mounted archers. The crusaders had travelled three days past Dorylaeum when the nobles in Conrad's army became desperate. They demanded a council with Conrad and argued that the Crusade should turn back. Conrad agreed. The German crusaders turned around and began their humiliating retreat to Nicaea. They continued to be harassed by Turkish forces and were repeatedly tricked by the feigned retreats of the mounted archers. Conrad himself suffered a serious wound to the head from a Turkish arrow. At the beginning of November, the German army reached the relative safety of Nicaea. Many crusaders decided to return home leaving Conrad with a much-reduced and weakened force.

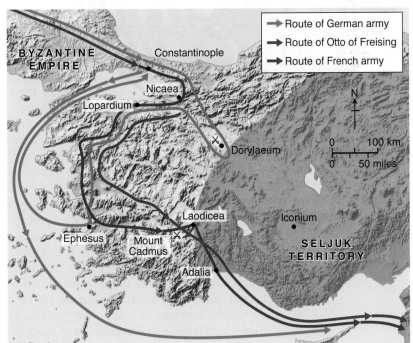

△ **Anatolia during the Second Crusade.**

■ Remember to add more events and issues to your factor folders.

Louis' march to Constantinople and into Asia Minor

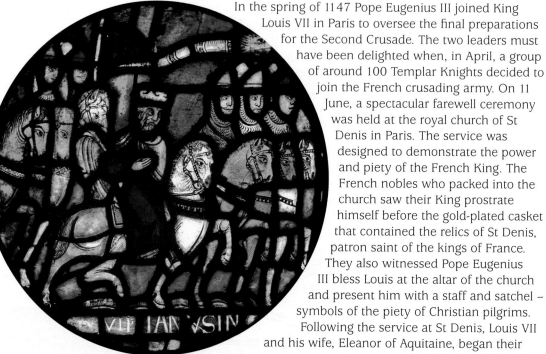

In the spring of 1147 Pope Eugenius III joined King Louis VII in Paris to oversee the final preparations for the Second Crusade. The two leaders must have been delighted when, in April, a group of around 100 Templar Knights decided to join the French crusading army. On 11 June, a spectacular farewell ceremony was held at the royal church of St Denis in Paris. The service was designed to demonstrate the power and piety of the French King. The French nobles who packed into the church saw their King prostrate himself before the gold-plated casket that contained the relics of St Denis, patron saint of the kings of France. They also witnessed Pope Eugenius III bless Louis at the altar of the church and present him with a staff and satchel – symbols of the piety of Christian pilgrims. Following the service at St Denis, Louis VII and his wife, Eleanor of Aquitaine, began their journey to the Holy Land. The King assembled the French forces, now tens of thousands strong, at Metz, and followed the same route to Constantinople as Conrad III. Odo of Deuil, Louis' chaplain, wrote a detailed account of the journey. He tells us that, at Metz, the King tried

△ A magnificent new stained-glass window to mark the start of the Second Crusade was especially commissioned for the church of St Denis. Some of the fourteen roundels in the window showed the heroic deeds of the first crusaders. Twelve of the roundels were destroyed in the French Revolution, but two survive in a museum in the USA. This scene shows a king leading his army into battle.

to ensure that discipline would be maintained by establishing clear rules of behaviour for his crusading army. The crusaders accepted the authority of the King and, at first, things went smoothly. However, lack of discipline became a problem when some of the pilgrims began to experience difficulties over supplies. According to Odo, Byzantine officials kept the King's own retinue well supplied with food, but the high prices charged by locals meant that many poorer pilgrims faced difficulties. Louis wrote to Abbot Suger asking him to send more funds, but this would obviously take time. More immediately, Louis was unable to stop crusaders from terrorising local market traders. Violence broke out. There were even fights between French crusaders and some stragglers from Conrad's army.

On 4 October, nearly four months after leaving Paris, Louis reached Constantinople. Manuel I feared and distrusted the French even more than the Germans. He was terrified that the combined armies of Roger II and

Louis VII might attack Constantinople. This fear was one of the reasons why Manuel I signed a peace treaty with the Seljuk Turks. Odo of Deuil's account makes it clear that there was an element in the French army that was particularly hostile towards the Byzantines. When they learned of Manuel's peace treaty with the Seljuk Turks they urged Louis to contact Roger and mount a joint attack on the Byzantine capital. Louis rejected their advice and entered Constantinople as the honoured guest of Manuel. During Louis' stay in Constantinople Manuel provided a lavish banquet for his entertainment and escorted him around the impressive palaces and churches of the city. Manuel also ordered that the majority of crusaders who remained outside the city should be provided with food at fair prices. But underlying Manuel's hospitality was a desire to divert the French away from Constantinople. He persuaded the French crusaders to cross the Bosphorus by spreading false rumours that the Germans were winning great victories in Asia Minor. He also agreed to provide the crusaders with guides and food markets on their journey to the Holy Land.

> ■ Add ideas and information to your factor folders.

Defeat at Mount Cadmus

Having crossed the Bosphorus and entered Asia Minor, French crusaders joined forces with what remained of Conrad's army and headed for the coastal town of Ephesus. Food supplies in local markets soon thinned out. It seems that Manuel had failed to ensure that local Greek officials provided the markets that he had promised. At Ephesus, Conrad decided that his injuries were too serious to continue. Manuel I invited him to spend the winter in Constantinople where he could be nursed back to health. In late December, heavy rains and snow sapped the morale of the crusaders. Louis decided to leave the coast, leading his army through the mountains and heading for Adalia, a major port in southern Asia Minor. The French crusaders faced constant attack from the Seljuk Turks. As they struggled along the high and narrow tracks of Mount Cadmus the French forces stretched out for six miles and became easy targets for the Turks. From their hidden positions behind trees and rocks, the Seljuk Turks fired volleys of arrows into the panic-stricken Christians and watched them fall to their deaths. According to Odo of Deuil, Louis VII only managed to escape by using tree roots to climb onto a rock from where he bravely fended off the enemy.

Shaken by the losses at Mount Cadmus, Louis handed over the running of the entire French army to the Knights Templar. This decision strengthened the discipline of the French crusading army, but weakened the authority of the King. Exhausted and hungry, the crusaders struggled into Adalia around 20 January. The King considered marching on, but was persuaded by his nobles to sail to Syria with his knights. Louis tried to ensure that the poor crusaders left behind were protected by the Byzantines, but most died of starvation or were killed during Turkish attacks. The French King reached Antioch in March 1148. Meanwhile, Conrad III having regained his health in Constantinople, sailed to Acre. Now both kings were in the Holy Land would it be possible to breathe new life into the Crusade?

> ■ Add more ideas and information to your factor files.
>
> In your opinion, which factors are most important in explaining the disasters that the Crusade experienced in Asia Minor?

War and defeat in Syria, March 1148 to July 1148

In March 1148, Louis VII, his wife Eleanor of Aquitaine and the surviving French nobles arrived in Antioch where they were warmly welcomed by Prince Raymond, Eleanor's uncle and ruler of Antioch. But behind the warm welcome lay a political agenda. Raymond knew that there was now little chance that the crusaders would attempt to retake Edessa. In 1146, the city had again been attacked by Muslim forces and now lay empty and in ruins. In any case, Raymond had always disliked Count Joscelin and saw no reason why he should encourage the crusaders to recover the city. Instead, Raymond hoped that the French forces would join him in a campaign to capture the Muslim cities of Aleppo and Shaizar. If these two cities could be brought under Christian control, his state of Antioch would become more secure. A crusader campaign in northern Syria would also help Raymond to shake off the power of the Byzantine Emperor who claimed lordship over this territory. In mid-May 1148, Raymond called an assembly to discuss his plan. You can imagine his horror and fury when Louis rejected his idea of a campaign in northern Syria.

Count Joscelin II was the ruler of Edessa. See page 72.

A number of reasons might explain why Louis chose not to support Raymond:

- The King's intense personal piety might have drawn him to Jerusalem where he could fulfil his pilgrim's vows by visiting the holy sites.
- He may have felt it was necessary to join forces with Conrad III whose forces had landed further south at Acre.
- His army was ill-equipped for siege warfare, lacking the foot-soldiers that would be needed to build siege engines and tunnels.
- His on-going financial difficulties may have led him to think that he would struggle to pay for a campaign.
- He may have been reluctant to attack cities in northern Syria over which, if the crusaders succeeded, the Byzantine Emperor could legitimately claim control.

◁ The marriage of Eleanor of Aquitaine and Louis VII from a fourteenth-century French manuscript. The rift between Louis and Raymond may have deepened because of gossip that Eleanor was involved in a sexual relationship with Raymond, who was her uncle. The evidence for this sex scandal is inconclusive, but it seems that rumours about the affair circulated at the time and they helped to poison the relationship between the crusaders and the ruler of Antioch.

Defeat at Damascus

By the early summer of 1148, the French and German crusading armies were together in the **Levant** for the first time. The western leaders and the rulers of the crusader states needed to consider their next move. On 24 June 1148 a grand council was held near Acre to decide on the future course of the Crusade. Louis and Conrad, together with their leading nobles and bishops, met with the young King of Jerusalem Baldwin III, his mother Melisende and the religious leaders of the crusader states. Various options were discussed, but the Christian leaders made the decision to attack the city of Damascus. Some earlier historians argued that this was a foolish move, but, more recently, the reasons for the decision to target Damascus have been better understood. From 1140, Unur, the ruler of Damascus, had allied his city with the Christian Kingdom of Jerusalem to combat the threat from Zengi. After Zengi's murder in 1146, Unur's relations with the new ruler of Aleppo (Zengi's son Nur ad-Din) improved. A treaty between the two Muslim rulers was sealed by a marriage between Nur ad-Din and Unur's daughter. The alliance between Unur and Nur ad-Din meant that, in the year before the Second Crusade, the military power of the Muslim forces in the Near East had grown in strength. Damascus now posed a real threat to the security of the crusader states.

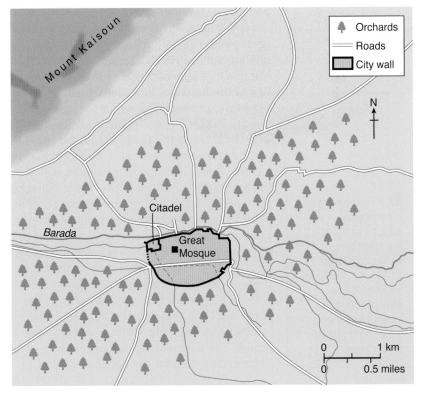

△ The Siege of Damascus, July 1148.

The city of Damascus lies on a flat plain overlooked to the north by Mount Kaisoun. In the twelfth century, the River Barada ran along the northern edge of the city's walls. The river fed a network of water channels that irrigated orchards which stretched for five miles beyond the walls of Damascus. The city's orchards provided a formidable defensive barrier. The orchards were made up of small plots surrounded by mud walls. Some plots had towers which the owners used to watch over their land. Fruit was carried into Damascus along narrow paths, wide enough only for small carts and pack animals, but not for an invading army. On Saturday 24 July, the combined forces of the crusader states and the armies of Conrad and Louis started to pick their way through the dense orchards to the south-west of the city. The Muslims used their local knowledge to attack the

Franks. They barricaded the paths, thrust spears and fired arrows through peep-holes in the mud walls and sent volleys of arrows into the Franks from their positions on the watch towers. The Franks lost many men, but pressed on. By the end of the first day, they had managed to establish a camp on the open ground in front of the city, from where they could access the water of the river.

Damascus now seemed vulnerable. For three days a desperate struggle ensued. The inhabitants of the city gathered in the Great Mosque where one of Damascus' sacred treasures, the Qu'ran owned by Caliph Uthman (a companion of the Prophet Muhammad who later became the third Caliph), was displayed. The people sprinkled their heads with ashes and prayed for divine help. Unur led a heroic and vigorous defence of the city. Playing for time, he ordered the inhabitants to barricade the streets with piles of rubble and sent messengers to Nur ad-Din requesting reinforcements. He also sent envoys to the Christian leaders, warning of Nur ad-Din's approach. Other messages were sent specifically to Baldwin III and the nobles of Jerusalem, pointing out that the western crusaders would want to keep Damascus for themselves if they managed to defeat the city. According to Christian sources, the Franks began to argue over who should have the rights to rule the city if it fell.

The Franks held a council of war on the evening of 27 July. They made a controversial decision to leave their well-watered camp and move to the east of the city from where a more direct attack on Damascus could be made. William of Tyre later claimed that the Damascenes had bribed some Jerusalem noblemen to persuade the Christian leaders to shift their position. Whether true or not, Conrad and Louis acted on the advice of the local Christians and switched the attack to the east of the city. The defences in this part of Damascus proved to be no weaker than in the west, and the Christians now found themselves in an exposed and waterless position. Hungry and thirsty in the blistering heat of summer, and fearful that they may be trapped between the city and Nur ad-Din's advancing armies, the Christian armies were forced into a humiliating retreat. The failure at Damascus finally destroyed the high hopes which Christendom held for the Second Crusade.

From blame to explanation

Given the high hopes which Christians held for the Second Crusade it is not surprising that people soon started pointing the finger of blame for its failure. Conrad III was clear about where the blame should lie. In a letter sent to his regent, Wibald, in the autumn of 1184, he focused on the treachery of Baldwin III and the Jerusalem nobility:

> Conrad, by the grace of God august King of the Romans, to the venerable abbot, Wibald of Corvey, sends his grace and good will.
>
> Because we know that you desire to have news of us, that is, of our prosperous state, we have thought fit to announce this to you first. By God's pity we are well. We have boarded our ships, due to return on the Feast of the Blessed Virgin in September. Everything that God has willed or the men of the land have permitted has been

■ From what you have discovered about events in the Holy Land between March 1148 and July 1148, you should be able to add quite a lot of ideas and information to your factor files.

done in these parts. To speak of the men: when we had gone to Damascus – a unanimous decision – and had fought hard to set up our camp before the city gate, it was almost certain that the city would be taken, but from a source we did not suspect, treachery arrived, for 'they' assured us that side of the city could not be taken. They purposely led us to another side where there was no water for the army and no obvious access. Angry and grieved they all returned, having achieved nothing.

■ What does Conrad's letter reveal about the troubled relations between the crusaders and the crusader states?

Conrad's focus on the betrayal and treachery of Baldwin III and the Jerusalem nobility was clearly intended to shift the focus of blame away from himself. Other sources blamed the western Kings for promising Damascus to Count Thierry of Flanders if it fell. As a western ruler of Damascus, Count Thierry would certainly have antagonised the leaders of the crusader states. In the aftermath of the Crusade some commentators directed their blame more widely, pointing to poor military leadership and the lukewarm support of the Byzantines in Asia Minor. Bernard of Clairvaux came in for severe criticism and the reputation of Pope Eugenius III also suffered. Most western sources overlooked the fact that the Muslim forces may have simply been too strong for the Christians. The people of Damascus were defending one of the holiest cities in the Islamic world. The determination of the Muslims to hold on to such an important spiritual centre had begun to unite the followers of Islam in the Near East. In the years following the Second Crusade the Muslim revival would intensify and the crusader states would be forced into a desperate struggle for survival.

■ Concluding your enquiry

It's time to sort out your factor folders. As you've seen, there was plenty of blame being bandied around after 1148! But the job of the historian is not to *blame*, but to *explain*. Your challenge now is to use the ideas and information you have collected in your factor folders to write an explanation of what, in your view, led to the failure of the Second Crusade for the Christians.

- Which factors do you think were most important in explaining the failure of the Crusade for the Christians?

- In what ways do some of the factors overlap?

- Use the points in your factor folders to produce a plan for a clear, well-structured and detailed explanation of why the Second Crusade failed.

Women and the Crusades

Historians think that this sculpture, made shortly after the Second Crusade, shows Hugh I Count of Vaudemont and his wife Aigeline of Burgundy. Hugh is clearly a crusader. He wears a cloak stitched with a crusader's cross, a pilgrim's purse hangs from his waist and he grips a pilgrim's staff in his right hand. As for Aigeline, it looks like she is giving her husband a hug. She presses her cheek against Hugh's head and her left hand lies across his middle. The sculpture is a puzzling one. It's hard to know whether Aigeline is saying goodbye to Hugh or welcoming him home. We can't be certain why the sculpture was made or what message it would give to people in the twelfth century. Does it show Aigeline's joy at the return of her husband or Hugh's determination to go on crusade despite his wife's pleas for him to stay? What other emotions might be expressed in the sculpture: love, sadness, distress, pride, sacrifice, devotion, piety? It's hard to be certain.

△ A sculpture of a crusader and his wife originally in the Priory of Belval, France.

One thing we can be sure about is that, like most women, Aigeline did not accompany her husband on crusade. Medieval Europe was a male-dominated society and the Crusades were seen as men's business. From the Church's perspective, women were a hindrance in a crusading army. They might slow down the Crusade and could cause problems if taken captive. A crusade was a holy pilgrimage and crusaders were supposed to abstain from sex during their journey to the Holy Land. If women were allowed on crusade, they could inhibit the spiritual purity of the crusaders. The Church therefore banned single women from taking the cross and even discouraged wives from accompanying their husbands. The only women who accompanied the Crusades with the blessing of the Church were washerwomen who played an important role in preventing the spread of lice and were usually too old to provide sexual temptation.

Women who did not go on crusade still played an important role in the crusading movement. A crusader was temporarily unable to fulfil his marriage vow and therefore needed the consent of his wife to take the cross. From the beginning of the Crusades, the agreement of a wife to her husband's absence was crucial. In 1096, Urban II wrote that newly-married men, in particular, should seek the agreement of their wives before taking the cross, otherwise there was a danger that either husband or wife would break the marriage vow to be faithful to their spouse. Agreeing to a spouse becoming a crusader must have been agonising. Wives could expect to face several difficult years managing their husband's estates, raising children alone and worrying about the safety of their husband. Many women rose to the challenge, managing the household and estates very successfully.

Crusading women

The Church was not entirely successful in preventing women from going on crusade. Groups of single women sometimes travelled together and it was certainly not unknown for wives to accompany their husbands. Finding out about women's experience is difficult. Overall, there is little evidence about women in the accounts of chroniclers, but they do sometimes give us glimpses of women's experiences during individual crusades. Misogynistic chroniclers sometimes criticised women for causing logistical problems by using up supplies or slowing down the pace of the crusading army, but they also revealed that women fulfilled important roles on the journey to the Holy Land. Fetching water was a female task in twelfth-century Europe and this was a role frequently mentioned by the chroniclers. The preparation of food and provision of medical care were also important tasks performed by women.

You can find individual examples of women accompanying their husbands on pages 82 and 108.

This picture shows that medieval women could play an active role in warfare. The chronicles occasionally describe women using weapons during a siege although the descriptions cannot always be verified. William of Tyre mentioned that some women took up arms during the attack on Jerusalem in 1099. A chronicler of the Third Crusade wrote that women used knives to slit the throats of prisoners taken from a captured ship at the Siege of Acre. More frequently, chroniclers describe women's bravery in a supporting role. In 1187, Margaret of Beverley helped to defend the walls of Jerusalem against Saladin's forces by taking water to the men on the walls. For protection she wore a cooking pot as a helmet. Women were recorded helping with tasks such as carrying stones and earth to fill in moats so that siege engines could be pushed against town walls. It was dangerous work and women often met their deaths in this way. At the Siege of Acre one woman was admired by her fellow crusaders because her dying wish was for her corpse to be thrown into the ditch with the rocks and earth. Female acts of bravery were noted in some chronicles, but masculinity had to be kept intact and chroniclers usually made it clear that such women were transcending their gender.

Comment les dames de sete aleret uengier lo2 barons q lo2 fis q lo2 ...une roy ne repura quant elles fu rent uengies qlautre ronest engra

△ **Women besieging a tower.**

On the whole, chroniclers were more inclined to describe the problems that women caused on a crusade rather than to praise their bravery in battle. Adultery and prostitution seem to have been particular issues in crusading armies. Some chroniclers describe how, on occasions, prostitutes and other women were expelled from a crusader camp in order to win God's favour. Fulcher of Chartres recorded that at Antioch during the First Crusade both married and single women were expelled from the crusader camp in case their presence displeased the Lord. Such scenes remind us of the hardships that women were sometimes forced to endure during the Crusades.

6 What led to the Muslim recapture of Jerusalem in 1187?

Jerusalem, 2 October 1187. For the first time in almost 90 years the banners of Islam fluttered in the breeze above the city's battlements. Saladin, the Muslim leader, made his triumphant entrance into the city. This was a profoundly proud moment for Saladin. For the last thirteen years he had encouraged his fellow Muslims to follow the jihad and to recapture Jerusalem for Islam. Now, that goal had been achieved.

Saladin and his followers began a ritual cleansing of the Holy City. They climbed to the top of the Dome of the Rock and ripped down the large golden cross. They removed the Christian altar and statues from inside the building. They purified the Dome of the Rock and the Aqsa Mosque with rose water and incense. As part of the Muslim takeover of Jerusalem Saladin had a new minbar (pulpit) installed in the Aqsa Mosque. This rare black and white photograph is all that remains of Saladin's minbar. It stood in the Aqsa Mosque for 800 years until 1969 when it was destroyed in a fire.

The minbar that Saladin installed in the Aqsa Mosque was not new in 1187. It was in 1168 that the Muslim leader Nur ad-Din had commissioned the master carpenter al-Akharini to carve the finest minbar in the Muslim world. Nur ad-Din hoped that one day he would be able to install the wonderful minbar in the Aqsa Mosque in Jerusalem. For nearly twenty years the minbar had stood in the Great Mosque of Aleppo where it lay, according to one Muslim chronicler, 'like a sword in a scabbard' waiting for the day when the Muslims might achieve their dream of recapturing Jerusalem. In October 1187 that day had arrived.

△ The minbar of Nur ad-Din.

■ Enquiry Focus: What led to the Muslim recapture of Jerusalem in 1187?

One thing that the story of Nur ad-Din's minbar reveals is that the recapture of Jerusalem began a long time before 1187. Your challenge in this enquiry is to explain exactly what led to the Muslim recapture of Jerusalem in 1187. We have divided the period between the Second Crusade and the fall of Jerusalem into five different time-frames. Each of these can be seen as a 'step' towards the Muslim recapture of Jerusalem. We suggest that you start a separate page of notes for each of these steps.

In the middle of each page draw a 'step' to show which years it covers.

In the space above the 'step', make bullet point notes to summarise the achievements of Nur ad-Din or Saladin in these years.

In the space below the step, make bullet point notes to summarise changes in the crusader states in these years.

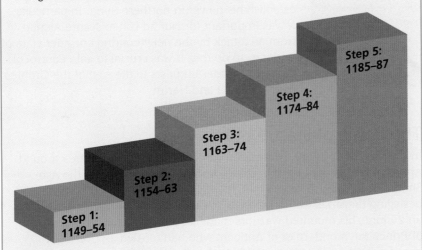

Step 1: 1149–54
Step 2: 1154–63
Step 3: 1163–74
Step 4: 1174–84
Step 5: 1185–87

At the end of the enquiry you can use your 'flight of steps' to consider a range of issues that shed light on the Enquiry Focus: *What led to the Muslim recapture of Jerusalem in 1187?*

- In what ways did Nur ad-Din lay the foundations for the Muslim recapture of Jerusalem?
- What particular strengths did Saladin display in the years leading up to the capture of Jerusalem?
- When and how did political weakness in the crusader states contribute to the fall of Jerusalem?
- Which turning points were particularly important in leading to the fall of Jerusalem?
- At what point do you think the Muslim recapture of Jerusalem became inevitable?
- Overall, what factors were most important in explaining what happened in 1187?

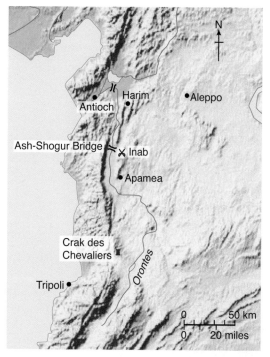

△ Northern Syria in 1150.

1149–54: Nur ad-Din and the crusader states

On the night of 14 September 1146, Zengi, lord of Mosul and Aleppo was knifed to death in his bed by one of his own servants. Zengi's heirs acted quickly. Saif ad-Din, his eldest son, took control of Mosul, the main centre of Sunni Islam. Nur ad-Din, Zengi's 28-year-old younger son, became the new emir of Aleppo. In the years that followed, Nur ad-Din would unite Syria, extend his power into Egypt and achieve a number of victories against the crusader states. However, at the beginning of his rule, Nur ad-Din's position was precarious. After the Second Crusade, he emerged as the most important Muslim leader in the Near East, but Nur ad-Din still needed to establish his power in northern Syria. In particular, it was important for Nur ad-Din to secure Aleppo from an attack by the neighbouring crusader state of Antioch. To do this, it was crucial to gain control of the two crusader outposts to the east of the Orontes river: Apamea and Harim.

The Battle of Inab, 1149

You have already encountered Nur ad-Din during the Second Crusade. See pages 85–86.

In the summer of 1149, Nur ad-Din's troops moved into the area around Apamea. He planned to isolate the town by taking control of the Ash-Shogur Bridge which crossed the River Orontes. Nur ad-Din began by besieging the small fort of Inab which protected the bridge. At daybreak on 29 June, his mounted warriors made a surprise attack on the forces of Prince Raymond, ruler of Antioch, who had formed an overnight encampment on the plain outside Inab. After hours of fighting in the heat and dust, Nur ad-Din's men emerged victorious. When the dust settled, they found the body of Raymond of Antioch among the dead. They decapitated Raymond and presented his head to Nur ad-Din who sent it as a trophy to the Caliph in Baghdad.

The Caliph was Nur ad-Din's spiritual leader.

Nur ad-Din's victory at the Battle of Inab allowed him to launch further attacks on crusader territory. In mid-July, his forces captured the town of Harim. By the end of July he had also taken Apamea. Nur ad-Din now controlled all the land to the east of the Orontes. However, he decided not to press home his victory by besieging the city of Antioch itself, perhaps realising that the city's huge fortifications, and the possibility of reinforcements from Jerusalem, made an attack too risky. Nur ad-Din's victory at Inab and his conquests of Harim and Apamea were enough to ensure that the crusader state of Antioch now posed a more limited threat to the security of Aleppo. In order to advertise the significance of his victory at Inab, Nur ad-Din bathed in the Mediterranean.

Weaknesses in the crusader states

In the years between 1149 and 1154 there were several reasons why the crusader states could offer only limited resistance to Nur ad-Din. The most important Latin ruler was Baldwin III, King of Jerusalem, but Baldwin faced some serious challenges.

1   In 1149 Baldwin was only nineteen years old. Since 1143 he had ruled jointly with his mother, Melisende, but, from 1149, relations with his mother soured because she refused to allow him to rule alone. Between 1150 and 1152 their relationship grew even worse as Baldwin tried to force Melisende's abdication and establish himself as an independent ruler.

2   From 1149 Baldwin III also faced the additional challenge of ruling Antioch. Prince Raymond's death at the Battle of Inab created a succession crisis in Antioch because his son and heir was only five years old. Constance, Raymond's young widow, refused to marry a man of Baldwin's choosing so this left Antioch without a male military commander. Baldwin III had no choice but to rule Antioch as well as Jerusalem.

3   Three years later, in 1152, Baldwin took over control of the County of Tripoli when Raymond II, ruler of Tripoli, was murdered by a band of assassins. This meant that Baldwin III was now charged with the rule of all three surviving crusader kingdoms. Baldwin III was a brave and competent ruler, but, in his early twenties, he was clearly stretched!

4   The young King received no help from Europe. Following the failure of the Second Crusade the Franks made urgent requests to European rulers for a new crusade, but there was no response. Baldwin III was left to defend the crusader states on his own.

Damascus, 1154

Despite these weaknesses, Nur ad-Din chose not to attempt a direct assault on the crusader states in the early 1150s. Instead, he focused his resources and energy on consolidating his power in Syria. Nur ad-Din's priority was to take control of the city of Damascus. In the four years between 1150 and 1154 he used a mixture of military threats and propaganda to subdue the city. His strategy worked: in April 1154, the people of Damascus surrendered. For the first time since the Crusades began, Aleppo and Damascus were now under the rule of one man. Nur ad-Din had created a united Muslim Syria. This would give him a formidable power base in his fight against the Franks.

Some medieval Muslim chroniclers suggested that from this point onwards, Nur ad-Din dedicated himself to jihad against the Franks, but the evidence does not support this view. Following his seizure of Damascus, Nur ad-Din agreed a truce with the crusaders that allowed him to continue securing his Syrian territory. Fighting a Holy War against the Christians of the Near East does not seem to have been at the top of Nur ad-Din's agenda in 1154.

■ Make your notes for the first step, 1149–54. Remember – the bullet points above the step should summarise Nur ad-Din's achievements and the bullet points below the step should summarise the changes in the crusader states.

Start with the main points. For Nur ad-Din's achievements these could be his securing of Aleppo and his victory over Raymond of Antioch. For the crusader states, the main points might be the problems of leadership and the lack of support from overseas. When you have decided on the main points you can then add the details.

1154–63: Nur ad-Din and the building of jihad

Nur ad-Din may not have been ready to fight a Holy War in 1154, but he was keen to portray himself as a devout Muslim and a warrior for jihad. The Muslim leader brought together the religious and military classes in Syria by ensuring that his army included religious men: prayer leaders, preachers, judges and **Sufi** mystics. He also saw it as his religious duty to construct buildings in the name of Islam. In the years between 1154 and 1163, Nur ad-Din paid for a range of new religious buildings in Damascus and other Syrian towns. Many of his new mosques, minarets, madrasas (religious schools), hospitals, orphanages and Sufi cloisters had his name inscribed on their walls. In 1163 Nur ad-Din completed the greatest of his buildings in Damascus – the House of Justice. It was here that his subjects could bring their grievances and where Nur ad-Din himself sometimes acted as judge. Nur ad-Din was keen to project an image of being a 'just ruler'. His House of Justice, and the other buildings that he sponsored, helped to portray him as a model Sunni Muslim ruler who was deeply religious and seriously committed to jihad.

In 1157–58, Nur ad-Din became seriously ill and almost died. This seems to have deepened his religious commitment. The Muslim chroniclers tell us that Nur ad-Din experienced a spiritual awakening in these years. After his illness he focused on his own greater jihad in preparation for Holy War (lesser jihad) against the Christians. Nur ad-Din discarded his luxurious clothes and began to wear the simple garments of a Sufi mystic. In 1161 he performed the **Hajj**, the pilgrimage to Islam's holiest city – Makkah. Following his pilgrimage he rebuilt the walls of Medina – Islam's second holiest city. At the same time as Nur ad-Din was becoming more deeply spiritual, religious leaders in Syria were stressing the importance of religious martyrdom. They wrote and preached that Muslims who died fighting the infidel would be rewarded with a place in Paradise. In particular, the religious leaders emphasised that it was the duty of good Muslims to recapture Islam's third holiest city – Jerusalem.

The crusader states fight back

After 1154, Nur ad-Din established himself as a devout Sunni ruler, but he made little real advance in jihad against the Franks. During the period 1154–63, the crusader states were beginning to regain some of their strength:

■ King Baldwin III proved to be more than a match for Nur ad-Din. In 1153 Baldwin had achieved an important victory when, after an eight-month siege, his armies had taken the southern port of Ascalon. This helped to secure the southern frontier of the crusader states and provided the crusaders with a potential stepping-stone into Egypt. The crusaders now held all the ports on the coast of Palestine, providing greater security for trade and pilgrimage.

■ In the north, the crusader state of Antioch began to revive. In 1153, after four years of ruling alone, Constance finally married a young and handsome French knight, Reynald of Châtillon. Reynald had fought alongside Baldwin in the Siege of Ascalon and had gained the King's permission to marry Constance. He was a particularly brutal man who proved to be a formidable defender of crusader territory until he was captured by Nur ad-Din in 1161.

- In 1158 the crusaders recaptured the town of Harim from Nur ad-Din. Antioch was on the offensive again.

- The crusader states were further strengthened when relations with the Byzantines were restored. By the late 1150s, the Byzantine Emperor, Manuel I, was keen to forget the bad feeling caused by the Second Crusade. In September 1158, Baldwin III married Manuel's niece, Theodora. Three years later, Manuel married Maria of Antioch, the daughter of Constance and her first husband, Prince Raymond. These marriage alliances brought the Byzantines and the Franks closer together.

Nur ad-Din's pragmatism

In the light of these changes, Nur ad-Din proved himself to be a pragmatic ruler. In 1159, when Manuel I assembled Christian armies in Antioch for an assault on Aleppo, Nur ad-Din knew that the Muslims were outnumbered, so he negotiated a truce. In 1161, the capture of Reynald of Châtillon weakened the principality of Antioch, but Nur ad-Din chose not to exploit this. Instead, he agreed a truce with Baldwin III. In 1163, Baldwin III died suddenly of consumption at the age of 33. With the death of their most powerful ruler the crusader states were vulnerable, but, once again, Nur ad-Din did not react. In the years 1154–63, Nur ad-Din might have experienced a spiritual awakening and laid the foundations for jihad, but he chose not to commit his forces to a Holy War against the crusader states. In 1163, all that was about to change.

> ■ Make your notes for the second step, 1154–63. Above the step, summarise the main achievements of Nur ad-Din during these years. Below the step, explain how the Franks regained some of their strength.
>
> To what extent do you think the recapture of Jerusalem had become more likely by 1163?

1163–74: Conflict and control in Egypt

After 1163, Nur ad-Din began to confront the Franks on the borders between his territory in Syria and the crusader states of Antioch, Tripoli and Jerusalem. However, the main focus of conflict in these years was in Egypt. Nur ad-Din knew that division between his Sunni Syria and Shi'ah Egypt was undermining any hope of recapturing Jerusalem and of forcing the Franks out of the Near East. If he could gain control of Egypt and unite Damascus with Cairo, the crusader states would be encircled. Control of Egypt would also give Nur ad-Din access to the country's fantastic wealth. Egypt's Fatimid regime had been weak for many years and, in 1163, it was in chaos. The summary of events on pages 96 and 97 shows how Nur ad-Din and his generals gained control of Egypt in the years between 1163 and 1174.

△ Egypt and Palestine in the twelfth century.

Gaining control of Egypt, 1163–74

September 1163, Amalric, King of Jerusalem, invaded Egypt, but retreated

Baldwin III had no children and was therefore succeeded by his 27-year-old brother Amalric. William of Tyre, the new King's chancellor, wrote that Amalric was quite tall and good-looking with blond hair and a full beard. He was confident but quieter than his brother, perhaps because of a slight stammer. Amalric did not eat or drink too much, but was very fat 'with breasts like those of a woman hanging down to his waist'. Like Baldwin, Amalric would prove to be a strong crusader king who was prepared to confront his enemies. From the beginning of his reign, the new King of Jerusalem made the conquest of Egypt a priority. He invaded Egypt for the first time in September 1163 and began to besiege the town of Bilbais which lay on a tributary of the Nile. His troops were forced to retreat when the Egyptians opened the dykes and flooded the land around the town. However, before his death in 1169, Amalric would attempt four more invasions of Egypt.

April 1164, Nur ad-Din's forces invaded Egypt

During 1164, Nur ad-Din's energy was directed at fighting the Franks in the north, but he knew that he could not risk the possibility of a Frankish victory in Egypt. Reluctantly, his attention was drawn to the south. In April 1164, he ordered his Kurdish general, Shirkuh, to lead a campaign into Egypt. Shirkuh, blind in one eye and immensely fat, was feared and respected as a veteran soldier. Shirkuh was a trusted member of Nur ad-Din's inner circle, but he saw an Egyptian invasion as an opportunity to establish independent power for his own clan, the Ayyubids. Shirkuh's second-in-command was his young nephew, Yusuf Ibn Ayyub, better known as Salah ad-Din or Saladin. Between 1164 and 1169 Shurkuh and Saladin fought a number of bitter campaigns against the crusaders in the Nile region. Increasingly, they saw the potential of establishing an Ayyubid kingdom in Egypt.

January 1169, Shirkuh gained control of Egypt

The Egyptian wars came to a head in the winter of 1168–69. The Franks' fourth invasion of Egypt, which began in October 1168, was a disaster. Amalric managed to capture the town of Bilbais, but failed to besiege Cairo and was forced to retreat from Egypt. The stage was now clear for Shirkuh. In January 1169, he ordered the assassination of the Egyptian vizier and made himself the new ruler of Egypt. With Syria and Egypt now united under the banner of Sunni Islam, the threat to Jerusalem, and to the overall security of the crusader states, suddenly intensified.

◁ A late medieval depiction of al-Malik al-Nasir Salah al-Dunya wa'l-Did Abu'l Muzzafar Yusuf Ibn Ayyub Ibn Shadi al-Kurdy – known (thankfully) to westerners as Saladin. In his twenties, Saladin had been Nur ad-Din's favourite polo partner. In 1169, when he took over from his uncle in Egypt, he was 31 years old. According to one Muslim chronicler, Saladin's religious conviction deepened after his rise to power. He was said to have given up wine-drinking and other frivolities.

March 1169, Saladin established his power in Egypt

Within weeks of taking control of Egypt, Shirkuh, by then in his sixties and vastly overweight, died of a heart attack. He was succeeded as vizier by his nephew, Saladin. At first, Saladin's position seemed insecure, but he soon began to impose his authority. He appointed members of his own family to senior positions in the government. His father, for example, became treasurer of Cairo. Saladin also began to impose Sunni Islam on Egypt. He built Sunni madrasas, dismissed Shi'ah judges and began to destabilise the teenage Fatimid Caliph, al-Adid. Saladin defeated the Fatimids' powerful Sudanese infantry regiment and created his own military corps – the Salahiyya. In the autumn of 1169, at the coastal city of Damietta, Saladin defeated Amalric's fifth and final invasion of Egypt.

September 1170–March 1171, Amalric sought help from Europe and the Byzantines

The Syrian Muslims' acquisition of Egypt caused panic in the crusader states. In the autumn of 1170 Amalric sent diplomats to Europe to ask for help. Meetings with the Pope came to nothing. Political differences between King Louis VII of France and King Henry II of England (Amalric's nephew) meant that the two rulers could not agree on support for the crusader states. It was clear that there would be no new crusade to the Holy Land. With no prospect of help from European monarchs, Amalric travelled to Constantinople and paid homage to the Byzantine Emperor in the hope that Manuel I would help to defend the crusader states. Almalric's submission to the Byzantine Emperor showed how dangerous the threat from the Muslims had become by 1171.

September 1171 Saladin took control

By 1171 Saladin had tightened his grip on Egypt; but, as vizier, he was still second in command to the twenty-year-old Shi'ah Caliph, al-Adid. He was also bound by ties of loyalty to Nur ad-Din. At the end of August 1171 al-Adid became ill. A Muslim chronicler later claimed that he was poisoned. On Friday 10 September, Saladin took the next step in establishing his power and authority. On that day, for the first time in over 200 years, Friday prayers in Egypt's mosques omitted the Shi'ah Caliph's name, replacing it with that of the Sunni Caliph of Baghdad. The next day, Saladin presided over a huge military parade in Cairo. The message was clear: Saladin was now in control. With the death of the Caliph on 13 September, Shi'ah Egypt came to an end. In late September 1171, Saladin took his forces into Transjordan (see the map on page 100) intending to join Nur ad-Din in attacking the crusader castles of Montreal and Kerak. However, Saladin soon retreated to Egypt and the two armies never combined. Nur ad-Din became increasingly aware that he was losing control of Saladin. Tensions between the two Muslim leaders deepened. Nur ad-Din now threatened to invade Egypt.

May–July 1174, the deaths of Nur ad-Din and Amalric

By the spring of 1174 open warfare between Nur ad-Din and Saladin seemed imminent. Then, suddenly, on 15 May 1174, Nur ad-Din died of a heart attack. His body was later interred in one of the madrasas he had built in Damascus. During the 28 years of Nur ad-Din's rule, Aleppo and Damascus had been united, and the idea of jihad against Islam's enemies in the Near East had been revived. However, in 1174, the crusader states remained unconquered and Jerusalem was still under crusader control. Less than two months after Nur ad-Din's death, the crusaders' grip on Jerusalem began to look much less secure. On 11 July 1174, Amalric died following an attack of dysentery. He was succeeded by his son, Baldwin IV. Not only was Baldwin IV only thirteen years old, but he was also suffering from leprosy.

■ Make your notes for the third step, 1163–74. In what ways did the conflict in Egypt make the recapture of Jerusalem more likely?

1174–84: Crisis and conflict in the crusader states

In the summer of 1174, the contrast between the leaders of the Muslim and Frankish worlds in the Near East could not have been greater. Saladin was an experienced and ambitious warrior who was determined to impose his authority on the Muslim Near East. Baldwin IV was a thirteen-year-old boy with an incurable disease who could only rule through a regent. In the years between 1174 and 1184, Saladin secured his hold over Egypt and Syria and began to create a greater degree of unity among the Muslims of the Near East. Meanwhile, the crusader states became weaker and more divided. But how much closer did the Muslims come to recapturing Jerusalem over these years?

Saladin and the Muslim Near East

Saladin faced a tricky situation in 1174. With the death of Nur ad-Din the Zengid regime fractured, but members of the Zengid dynasty still held positions of power in Syria and **Mesopotamia**. In particular, Saladin knew that he would have to display loyalty to Nur ad-Din's young son, al-Salih. Saladin established his control over Syria through patient diplomacy and propaganda rather than through force. One of the first things Saladin did following Nur ad-Din's death was to write to al-Salih, expressing his loyalty and reassuring the young ruler that he would protect al-Salih from his enemies. Saladin gained further authority and legitimacy by marrying Nur ad-Din's widow. Saladin was absolutely determined to pursue his own power in Syria and used the threat of force when necessary. But during the first years of Saladin's rule he was careful to establish his authority over other Muslims in the name of al-Salih, and in the wider interest of jihad against the Franks.

Saladin began his bid to rule the Muslim Near East by targeting Damascus. He accused the Damascene rulers of weakness because they had agreed a truce with the crusader state of Jerusalem. On 28 October 1174, Saladin marched peacefully into Damascus. According to Muslim chroniclers, many people in the city rejoiced at Saladin's takeover. The large sums of money that Saladin distributed to the people of Damascus must have helped to win their support. He later justified his occupation of Damascus as a step on the road to retaking Jerusalem. Not everyone at the time was convinced by this explanation. Some people thought that Saladin's desire for Muslim unification was more to do with his personal ambition than his commitment to jihad.

By the end of 1174, several of Syria's warlords had decided to support Saladin. The Sultan was able to seize control of Homs, Hama and Baalbek with little bloodshed. The conquest of Aleppo proved more difficult – it was not until 1183 that Saladin finally brought Aleppo under his control. Like Nur ad-Din, Saladin had spent the first ten years of his rule mostly fighting other Muslims. Perhaps this was a necessary precondition to waging Holy War on the Franks and prizing Jerusalem from their grasp.

The vulnerability of the crusader states

During the reign of Baldwin IV (1174–85) the crusader states became less capable of countering Muslim attacks. The position of the Franks was not entirely hopeless. In 1177, for example, they defeated the Muslims and almost killed Saladin himself at Montgisard. But overall, the crusader states became more vulnerable between 1174 and 1185. The weakness of the crusader states was caused by three main factors.

1 **Baldwin IV's leprosy.** Baldwin proved to be a courageous and determined ruler, but, as he grew up, the King became more and more disabled. The fevers caused by Baldwin's leprosy sometimes made him incapable of ruling. By his early twenties Baldwin was partly paralysed and nearly blind. When on campaign, the King had to be strapped to a horse or carried in a litter. The longer Baldwin lived the weaker the crusader states became.

2 **Divisions within the ruling elite of the crusader states.** It was clear that Baldwin's reign would be short and that he would not produce an heir. Different factions within the crusader states therefore began to compete for power. Raymond III, Count of Tripoli (Baldwin's cousin), came to head one of the two main factions, while the other was led by Baldwin's mother, Agnes. In 1180, tensions between the two groups increased when Baldwin's sister, Sibylla, married Guy of Lusignan, a young French knight. Guy became a potential regent and successor to Baldwin, much to the disgust of Raymond's faction. This became a central issue in the politics of the crusader states and distracted the Franks from focusing on the threat from Saladin. When the Franks *did* turn their attention to Saladin, different approaches emerged. Raymond of Tripoli advocated truces with the Muslims but Reynald of Châtillon (after his release from prison in 1176) provoked Saladin with his aggressive campaigns.

3 **Lack of support from the Byzantine Empire and Europe.** We have seen how the crusader states were strengthened by a closer relationship with the Byzantine Empire during the reign of Manuel I. In 1180, the Byzantine Emperor died and the new Emperor, Andronicus I, showed little interest in supporting the Latin rulers of the Near East. Neither did European monarchs. In autumn 1184 three of the most important men in the crusader states – the Patriarch of Jerusalem and the masters of the Hospitallers and Templars – were sent to Europe seeking support, but neither Philip II of France nor Henry II of England felt able to lead a new crusade to the Holy Land. The three diplomats returned to Jerusalem empty-handed.

Confrontations and conflicts

The map below shows the main conflicts between the crusaders and the Muslims in the years between 1174 and 1184.

- Use the map and the previous two pages to make notes for the fourth step, 1174–84.
- Do you think that the weakness of the Franks was the most important change between 1174 and 1184?
- How much closer do you think the Muslims came to recapturing Jerusalem in these years?

2 Summer 1179: Baldwin IV had begun to build a castle at Jacob's Ford – an important crossing point on the River Jordan which separated Christian Palestine and Muslim Syria. Saladin could not ignore this as the castle was a threat to Damascus itself. In August 1179 the Muslims attacked Jacob's Ford and razed the castle to the ground.

1 Autumn 1177: Saladin launched his first military campaign on the crusader states. This was a limited raid rather than a full-scale invasion aimed at recapturing Jerusalem. Saladin's forces were defeated by Baldwin IV and Reynald of Châtillon at the Battle of Montgisard. Saladin was forced to flee for his life and was deeply humiliated.

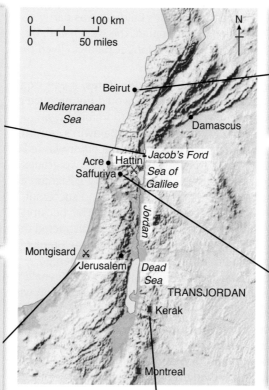

3 Summer 1182: Saladin launched a sea-borne attack on the crusader port of Beirut using the Egyptian navy that he had rebuilt. The Franks resisted and Saladin was forced to withdraw.

4 October 1183: Provoked by Reynald of Châtillon's attacks on Muslim pilgrims as they travelled across the Red Sea on their way to Makkah, Saladin launched a major offensive on the Kingdom of Jerusalem. He encountered crusader armies at Saffuriya, but failed to engage Guy of Lusignan's forces in battle and withdrew after a couple of weeks.

5 November 1183: Saladin besieged the crusader castle of Kerak in Transjordan. The attack coincided with the wedding celebration of Sibylla's younger sister, Princess Isabella. Saladin ordered his men to avoid bombarding the bridal suite for one night! More importantly, the castle resisted and Saladin's attack failed.

1185–87: The final step to Jerusalem

A turning point for Saladin

At the beginning of December 1185, Saladin, by now aged 48, became ill with a fever. As the weeks passed, Saladin failed to recover and his family became increasingly concerned. His Syrian doctors tried a range of treatments, but nothing worked. As the weeks turned into months, Saladin became weaker and weaker. In January, Saladin made his will. People began to think about the consequences of his death. Then, towards the end of February, Saladin began to regain his strength and to make a slow but lasting recovery. He spent most of the year of 1186 convalescing in Damascus – thinking, debating, hunting and hawking.

Many people came to see Saladin's illness during the winter of 1185–86 as a turning point in his life that had profound consequences on the future of the crusader states. Chroniclers suggested that Saladin's illness had forced him to confront his own mortality. From 1186, his spirituality deepened and he dedicated himself to the cause of jihad and to the recovery of Jerusalem. Since 1169, Saladin had been devoted to extending his authority over Egypt, Syria and parts of Mesopotamia. He had forged his Ayyubid Empire in the name of jihad in order to liberate the Holy City. Now it was time to focus on the end rather than the means. From 1186, Saladin became more determined to recapture Jerusalem and to expel the Franks from Palestine.

A succession crisis in the crusader states

Baldwin IV finally died in May 1185 at the age of just 23. He had shown great courage in enduring his leprosy, but his reign had created great instability in the crusader states. The turmoil only deepened after his death. The new King of Jerusalem was Baldwin V, the seven-year-old sickly child of Baldwin IV's sister, Sibylla. By September 1186, the young King was dead. A bitter dispute over the succession erupted in the crusader states. Raymond III, Count of Tripoli, who had been acting as regent, plotted to seize the throne. But Sibylla and Guy of Lusignan outmanoeuvred him and were crowned Queen and King of Jerusalem.

Many people considered Guy to be too weak and inexperienced to be King of Jerusalem. Raymond of Tripoli, in particular, was infuriated by Guy's elevation to the position of king. When Raymond discovered that Guy was planning to seize his lands in Galilee, Raymond made a truce with Saladin, allowing the Muslims to move across his lands if they would support him in his bid to be king. That Raymond, Count of Tripoli, one of the most important Frankish nobles, made such a pact with Saladin demonstrated the degree of disunity in the crusader states in 1186. One Muslim chronicler later noted:

> Their unity was disrupted and their cohesion broken. This was one of the most important factors that brought about the conquest of their territories and the liberation of Jerusalem.

The Battle of Hattin, July 1187

In the winter of 1186–87 Saladin began to prepare for a major offensive against the Franks. He was provoked by Reynald of Châtillon who raided a Muslim caravan that was crossing Transjordan on its way from Cairo to Damascus. Reynald's action contravened the truce with Saladin, but he refused to pay compensation. Saladin now had an excuse to fight. When the truce with the Franks expired in April 1187, he began to gather his forces for an invasion of Palestine. Saladin then launched a series of initial raids into crusader territory. On 1 May he easily overwhelmed a small force of Templar and Hospitaller knights at the Battle of Cresson. Saladin's forces withdrew carrying the heads of the slaughtered Christian soldiers on their spears. The loss of over 100 of the Franks' finest knights must have been a severe blow to their morale.

By June 1187, both sides had gathered their troops for battle. Saladin's aggression had persuaded Raymond of Tripoli to expel the Muslims from his territory and to support King Guy. The Christian army that assembled at Saffuriya probably numbered about 16,000 including around 1200 knights. They were heavily outnumbered by Saladin's forces which included at least 12,000 cavalry and probably totalled around 30,000. In the intense heat of the summer, the light armour of the Muslim warriors gave them an additional advantage over the heavily-armoured Franks. On 27 June 1187, Saladin led his men across the River Jordan just south of the Sea of Galilee. The full-scale Muslim invasion of Palestine had begun.

Saladin's aim was to draw the Franks away from Saffuriya and to engage them in a battle at a place of his choosing. On 2 June, Saladin laid his trap for the Franks by attacking the town of Tiberias. Raymond of Triploli's wife was besieged in the citadel, but Raymond advised King Guy to avoid a confrontation hoping that Saladin would retreat after capturing Tiberias and that a ransom could be paid for his wife. Guy rejected Raymond's advice and, on the morning of 3 July, ordered his army to march out from Saffuriya. This decision would ultimately end the Franks' 90-year occupation of the holy city of Jerulasem.

Tiberias was a day's march from Saffuriya across a dry and barren plateau. By leaving Saffuriya the Franks were abandoning their only certain supply of water. Saladin understood that access to water would play a crucial role in the conflict. He ordered all the wells in the area to be filled in, ensuring a plentiful supply of water for his own troops from the springs at Kafr Sabt and from supplies carried by camels from the Jordan valley. As Guy's men began to dehydrate, Saladin used his superior number of cavalry to attack them.

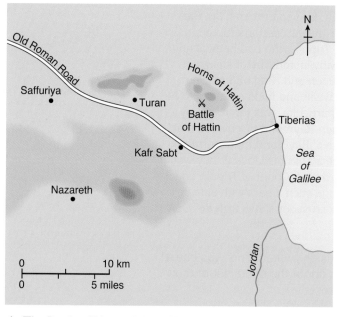

△ The Battle of Hattin, July 1187.

His mounted archers fired countless arrows into the Franks and claimed many lives. Guy realised that it was no longer possible to reach Tiberias that day and decided to make an overnight camp on the plateau.

As dawn broke over the hills of Galilee on 4 July, the thirsty and exhausted Christian soldiers set out along the old Roman road leading to Tiberias. Saladin waited until the blistering heat in the middle of the day before he made a move. Then he ordered his men to set fire to the dry scrub that lay ahead of the Franks. Guy's men were forced to make their way through clouds of hot and stifling smoke. Around noon, Saladin ordered his archers to unleash a torrent of arrows on the choking Franks. In desperation, Guy headed off the road and led his men to the crater of an ancient volcano known as the Horns of Hattin. Here the Franks found some temporary shelter from the Muslim bombardment.

△ The Horns of Hattin. This was the rocky outcrop in western Galilee where Saladin's forces defeated the Franks on 4 July 1187.

The King pitched his tent and rallied his men around the relic of the True Cross that had been discovered in the days after the capture of Jerusalem in 1099. Their only hope was to charge down the hill and try to kill Saladin himself. They made two attempts and killed many of the soldiers surrounding Saladin, but, each time, the Muslims forced them back into the crater. When Saladin saw Guy's red tent crumple he knew that the battle had been won. His soldiers brought him the Christians' True Cross. Saladin dismounted from his horse, prostrated himself on the ground in thanks to God and wept for joy.

After the battle, Saladin ordered the captured King Guy and Reynald of Châtillon to be brought to his tent. Guy was dying of thirst and shaking with fear. Saladin gave Guy a refreshing cup of iced water. This was a sign that the King's life would be spared. But Saladin did not allow Guy to pass the cup to Reynald. The Sultan had not forgotten Reynald's attacks on Muslim pilgrims and his raid on the Muslim caravan. Saladin drew his scimitar sword and sliced off Reynald's head.

Jerusalem

The huge army that had been assembled to confront Saladin in the summer of 1187 had left very few soldiers to defend the crusader settlements. In the weeks after the Battle of Hattin it is not surprising that Saladin's armies swept through the crusader states. His forces quickly recaptured the crusader coastal settlements in Palestine, and, by late September, they began to besiege their ultimate goal – Jerusalem. The Holy City was recaptured by the Muslims on 29 September after a five-day siege. Saladin made his triumphant entry into the city on 2 October – the anniversary of the Prophet's Night Journey from Jerusalem to heaven.

■ Make your notes for the final step. In your bullet point list above the step include all the factors that led to Saladin's success at Hattin. Below the step, make sure your bullet point list includes all the Frankish weaknesses that led to their defeat.

■ Concluding your enquiry

Now use your 'flight of steps' to consider the range of issues in the Enquiry Focus on page 91.

7 The Third Crusade, 1187–92

In the autumn of 1187, when news of Saladin's victory at Hattin and his recapture of Jerusalem began to reach Europe, people were deeply shocked. The elderly and frail Pope, Urban III, was said to have died of grief when he heard what had happened. In late October 1187, his successor, Pope Gregory VIII, issued the bull *Audita Tremendi* calling for a new crusade to the Holy Land. *Audita Tremendi* described the horrors of the Battle of Hattin and detailed the atrocities committed by Muslims. It blamed the calamity on the sins of the Franks in the crusader states, but insisted that Christians living in Europe were also guilty. Across Europe, people were deeply moved by the powerful call for repentance in Gregory's bull. The massive response to *Audita Tremendi* became the Third Crusade.

Richard's nickname 'the Lionheart' came from a fourteenth-century story which described Richard as capable of reaching down a lion's throat and tearing out its heart.

Two great historical figures have dominated the story of the Third Crusade: Saladin and Richard the Lionheart. Ever since the twelfth century, the Crusade has often been represented as a personal duel between the two leaders. The picture below shows Richard and Saladin locked in single combat. This scene is a fiction. Richard and Saladin never actually encountered each other face-to-face, though, as you'll discover, their armies clashed several times during the course of the Third Crusade.

▷ An illustration from the fourteenth-century Luttrell Psalter showing Richard I in single combat with Saladin.

Before you study the Third Crusade in detail it will help to gain an overview of key people, places and events. The summary on the next page will get you started.

- Who were the main people involved?
- Which places were particularly important in the Third Crusade?
- What were the major turning points of the Crusade?
- Did the Crusade succeed?

The Third Crusade: The essentials

1 Preparation

October 1187: Pope Gregory VIII issued the bull *Audita Tremendi*

November 1187: Richard, Count of Poitou and Duke of Aquitaine (later King Richard I of England), took the cross

January 1188: King Henry II of England and King Philip II of France took the cross

March 1188: Frederick Barbarossa, Emperor of Germany, took the cross

July 1189: Henry II died and was succeeded by his son, Richard

2 Journeys to the Holy Land

May 1189: Frederick and his armies left Germany and began their overland journey to the Holy Land

June 1189: Saladin released Guy, King of Jerusalem, from prison. In August, King Guy began the Siege of Acre which lasted for two years

10 June 1190: Frederick Barbarossa drowned

July 1190: Philip and Richard set out for the Holy Land from Vézelay in France

September 1190: Richard reached Sicily and decided to wait until the following spring to sail to the Holy Land

April 1191: On his way to the Holy Land Richard took the opportunity to invade Cyprus

8 June 1191: Richard arrived in the Holy Land

3 Crusader successes

12 July 1191: Richard and Philip captured the port of Acre, a major boost for the crusaders

3 August 1191: Philip abandoned the Third Crusade and returned to France

20 August 1191: Richard ordered the massacre of the Muslim prisoners at Acre

25 August 1191: Richard led the crusading army from Acre down the coast to Jaffa

7 September 1191: Richard's army defeated Saladin's forces at the Battle of Arsuf, an important victory for the crusaders

4 Attempts on Jerusalem

October 1191–January 1192: The crusaders attempted to take Jerusalem

June–July 1192: The crusaders made a second attempt to take Jerusalem, but retreated

1 August 1192: Saladin attacked Jaffa, but was defeated by the crusaders. This resulted in a stalemate

2 September 1192: The Treaty of Jaffa was signed bringing an end to the Third Crusade. There was no clear victor

9 October 1192: Richard I left the Holy Land

■ Enquiry Focus: What makes a good historical question about the Third Crusade?

This enquiry on the Third Crusade is different from the others in this book because we've decided not to include an overall enquiry question to focus your thinking. One of the challenges of studying history is to ask good questions about past events; so, at the end of this enquiry, it will be up to you to decide what makes a good historical question about the Third Crusade. In the meantime, as you find out more about the Crusade, you can do two things to help you think about possible enquiry questions:

1 Construct an annotated timeline of the key events of the Third Crusade. Include a summary of each event and explain what made it a turning point in the Crusade.

2 Make notes about four key issues that historians think shaped the Third Crusade:

- The leadership of Richard I
- The rivalry between Richard I and Philip II
- Challenges facing the crusaders
- The leadership of Saladin

Politics and preparations

The Third Crusade was led by the three most powerful monarchs in the Latin West: Richard I, Philip II and Frederick I. This potentially gave the Crusade enormous strength. The kings inspired many of their nobles to take the cross, ensuring that the Third Crusade had widespread support. The three monarchs were also able to use their royal administrations to organise and finance their campaigns. However, a crusade led by kings had a serious weakness. Western monarchs had their own kingdoms to defend while they planned and fought a crusade. This had a disruptive effect on the Third Crusade, especially because of the rivalry between the Crusade's leaders.

> ■ Start your annotated timeline and your notes on the key issues.

Richard I (1157–99), King of England (1189–99)

Richard was the son of Henry II and Eleanor of Aquitaine (the former wife of Louis VII of France, see pages 6 and 84). In 1172, at the age of fifteen he became the duke of Aquitaine, a region in south-western France that formed part of his father's vast Angevin Empire. Richard was soon drawn into the disputes between the Angevin monarchy and the King of France. At twelve years old he had been betrothed to Alice, daughter of the French King, Philip II. However, no wedding took place as Henry preferred to use the prospect of a marriage to his son as a negotiating tool with the French. The lingering issue of Richard and Alice's marriage was compounded by Richard claiming land from the French kings and his constant arguments with his father, Henry II. Through the 1180s Richard was sometimes in confrontation with Philip II and, at other times, allied to Philip against his father.

In late November 1187, Richard was one of the first western princes to take the cross. This was an extraordinary decision given his need to defend the duchy of Aquitaine and to ensure his succession to the Angevin Empire when Henry II died. Maybe Richard's religious devotion and personal connection to the Holy Land lay behind his decision. He was, after all, the great grandson of Fulk of Anjou, King of Jerusalem, 1131–42. Richard may also have seen the Third Crusade as an opportunity to be remembered as a great warrior. When Henry II died in July 1189, Richard inherited his father's vast empire. He now had enormous resources with which to fight the Third Crusade. However, Richard's new status as head of the Angevin dynasty meant that his rivalry with the King of France became even more intense.

Following his accession to the English throne, Richard proved himself to be an efficient administrator who was able to generate huge resources for the Crusade. He imposed a special crusading tax on his subjects known as the 'Saladin Tithe' and sold vast amounts of land and property in order to raise money. Richard was said to have joked that he would sell London itself if he could find a buyer. This ruthless economic planning was all the more important because Richard decided to travel to the Holy Land by sea. Building and hiring ships was expensive, but the sea journey would be quicker than travelling overland. It also allowed Richard to eliminate poor and unarmed pilgrims from the Crusade because places on the ships were limited and had to be paid for. Richard's crusading army would be a disciplined fighting force. To emphasise this point the King introduced harsh penalties for misconduct during the Crusade: murderers were to be tied to the body of their victim and thrown overboard; a crusader who attacked someone with a knife would have his hands chopped off.

Philip II (1165–1223), King of France (1179–1223)

He was only 24 years old when he took the cross with King Henry II of England in January 1188, but Philip had already ruled France for eight years. Philip and Henry met at Gisors near Paris in an attempt to settle their differences. It was there that they heard an impassioned sermon from the Archbishop Joscius of Tyre in which Joscius described the disastrous situation in the crusader states. According to one chronicler, the sermon was accompanied by a miracle when the Cross of Christ appeared in the sky above the English and French kings. The two monarchs decided to set aside their enmity and lead a new crusade. Their armies would wear different coloured crosses (white for the English and red for the French) to distinguish them on the campaign. The new spirit of co-operation did not last long. By the end of March the kings were in conflict again over the disputed succession to the Angevin lands in France.

The rivalry between the French and Angevin kings continued after Richard came to the throne in 1189. Philip was six years younger than Richard, but was a far more experienced king, having ruled France for nearly a decade when Richard came to power. Richard was Philip's vassal for the Angevin lands he held in France (Normandy, Anjou and Aquitaine) but he ruled a more powerful realm than Philip and had far more money at his disposal. Richard set out on crusade with the most organised and best-resourced crusading army. Philip's army was far smaller and was not as well-equipped. This difference between the resources of the two monarchs would become an increasing source of irritation for Philip during the Third Crusade. The rivalry between Richard and Philip was intensified by their different personalities. Richard was politically astute, but was a man of action and warfare. Philip was more calculating and cautious, and was determined to ensure that going on crusade did not weaken his power within the French kingdom.

The mistrust between Philip and Richard meant that neither was willing to set out on crusade without a guarantee that the other would leave at the same time. Groups of crusaders under the command of nobles left England and France from the spring of 1189, but the rivalry between Philip and Richard meant that the departure of the main crusading armies was delayed by nearly a year.

Frederick I (1125–90), King of Germany (1152–90)

Frederick I, Emperor of Germany, was also known as Barbarossa – red beard. By the time of the Third Crusade, Frederick's beard must have been rather grey because he was then in his late sixties. Frederick had ruled the largest and wealthiest lands in Christendom for 36 years. He had brought the independent-minded barons of Germany under control and had reached an agreement with the papacy after decades of hostility and conflict. In wealth, resources and political power, Frederick far outstripped the Kings of England and France. Frederick Barbarossa had played a major role in the Second Crusade as second in command to his uncle, Conrad III. In 1188 he made the momentous decision to lead another crusade to the Holy Land.

Frederick took the cross at an assembly at Mainz in March 1188. According to one chronicler, many men were in tears as they listened to a reading of Pope Gregory's bull, *Audita Tremendi*. Frederick announced his intention of leaving in just over a year. He then began preparations for his departure, exiling his main political opponent and establishing his son as his heir in Germany. Frederick ensured that his own troops were properly funded, but insisted that individual nobles should pay for their own crusade. When Frederick set out from Germany in May 1189, he led a huge and well-equipped crusading army. Had it not been for a terrible accident, Frederick would surely have played a central role in the Third Crusade.

Developing problems – journeying to the Holy Land

On 4 July 1190 **Richard I and Philip II** set out from Vézelay. At Lyon their armies divided having arranged to rendezvous at Messina in Sicily. Before leaving Vézelay, Richard and Philip agreed to share any profits from the Crusade equally. This simple agreement would become a source of conflict as the Crusade progressed.

Richard reached Sicily in September 1190, one month after Philip. His Angevin army made an attack on Messina, ignoring the fact that Philip II was already lodged in the city. Richard spent six months in Sicily, gathering more money and resources, and organising his marriage to Berengaria, daughter of the King of Navarre. In return for 10,000 marks, Philip reluctantly absolved Richard of the longstanding obligation to marry his sister Alice, but this created further tension between the two leaders.

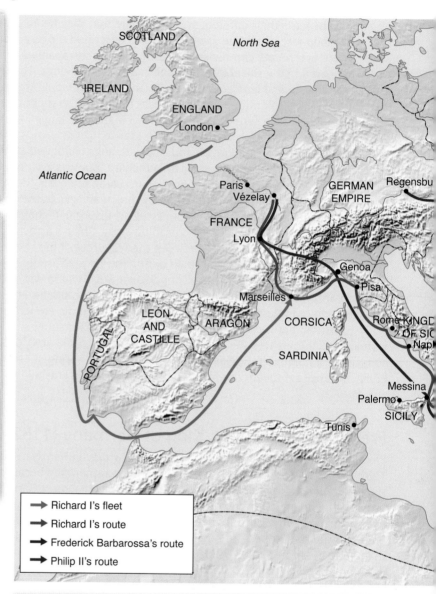

- → Richard I's fleet
- → Richard I's route
- → Frederick Barbarossa's route
- → Philip II's route

Richard left Sicily on 30 March 1191. Three days later, a gale scattered his fleet. The ship containing his sister Joan and his fiancé Berengaria was blown as far as the south coast of Cyprus. Isaac II, the Greek ruler of Cyprus, tried to capture the princesses. Richard seized the opportunity to invade Cyprus. He later sold the island to the Templars, but did not share the profits with Philip.

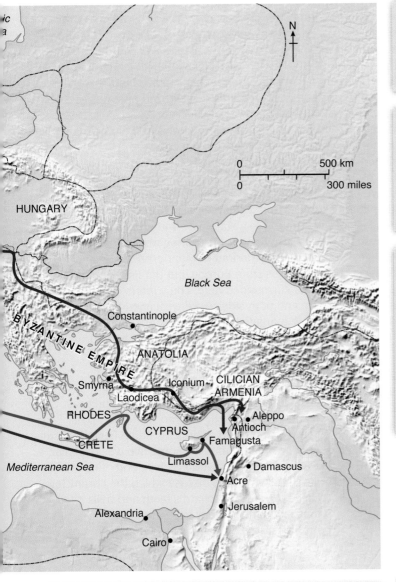

Frederick decided on an overland march to the Holy Land. He set out from Regensburg in May 1189 leading his forces through Hungary and then Byzantium.

The Byzantines agreed to help the crusaders with guides, markets and security, but feared that Frederick's army might attempt to conquer Byzantium. They failed to prevent attacks on the crusaders as they marched through Byzantium.

At the end of April, the German crusaders left Byzantium and entered the territory of the Seljuk Turks. As they lumbered through the Anatolian Hills they faced hunger, thirst and repeated ambushes. In mid-May 1190, Frederick's army reached the Seljuk capital of Iconium. In spite of their weakened state, the German crusaders took the city and continued southwards into Christian Armenia.

On 10 June 1190 Frederick drowned while trying to cross a river into Cilician Armenia. Frederick had died even before Richard and Philip had set out from Vézelay. This was a terrible blow to the Third Crusade. Many German knights returned home, but the remnants of Frederick's army continued to Acre.

Add to your annotated timeline and your notes on the key issues.

What made Frederick I's death such a terrible blow to the Third Crusade?

Victory at Acre, July 1191

Saladin's struggle

In the years following Saladin's great victories at Hattin and Jerusalem in 1187, his political and military strength began to decline. Divisions within the Muslim world resurfaced and Saladin struggled to take control of the remaining crusader strongholds. In the winter of 1187–88 Saladin attacked the crusader port of Tyre, but the town was successfully defended by Conrad of Montferrat, an Italian nobleman recently arrived in the Holy Land. Then, the following summer, Saladin released from prison Guy of Lusignan, King of Jerusalem. This was a costly decision. By August 1189, Guy gathered several thousand men and besieged Muslim-held Acre –one of the most important ports on the Mediterranean coast.

Guy positioned his troops on a low hill called Mount Toron, nearly a mile to the east of Acre. A swift attack from Saladin's more numerous troops could have finished the Franks, but he was too cautious and set up a holding position about six miles to the south-east of Acre. For the next year and a half, the Siege of Acre ground to a stalemate with the Franks camped in trenches between Saladin's army and the Muslim garrison inside Acre. The Christian forces were swelled by Conrad of Montferrat's men and then by the first waves of crusaders from Europe, but the Franks could not break the strong walls that surrounded Acre. The winters of 1189 and 1190 were particularly harsh, and both sides were weakened by disease and hunger. The city somehow managed to resist the Christian onslaught. However, by the summer of 1191, Sultan Saladin must have been dreading the arrival of the Kings of England and France.

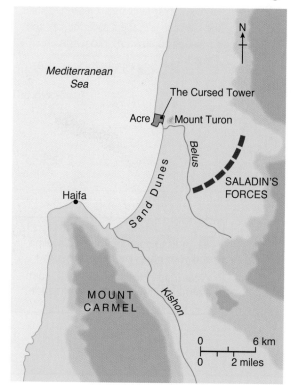

▽ The Siege of Acre.

Crusader victory

On 8 June 1191, Richard I landed on the coast near Acre with great ceremony. He set up his camp to the north of the city, Philip having taken up a position to the east some five weeks earlier. Within days of Richard's arrival, both kings were struck down with a disease which the chroniclers called 'Arnaldia'. Richard's teeth and nails loosened, and his hair began to fall out. Despite his illness, the Lionheart opened negotiations with Saladin. The English King even sent envoys to Saladin's camp requesting ice and fruit. This willingness to use diplomacy as well as military strength would be a crucial aspect of Richard's strategy during the Third Crusade. Saladin, too, was willing to negotiate, but thought it improper for kings to meet before an agreement had been reached.

In the end, bitter warfare rather than diplomacy determined the fate of Acre. In late June and early July the siege reached a climax with a hard-fought struggle between the siege engines, catapults, **sappers** and scaling ladders of the crusaders and the **Greek fire**, stone-throwing machines and counter-sappers of the Muslims. Philip's men directed their catapult on the Cursed Tower at Acre's north-eastern corner. Richard's troops constructed two well-designed catapults and bombarded the city with massive stones that they had brought from Messina. By 2 July, the incessant bombardment from the crusaders' siege machines began to pay off. The Cursed Tower was weakened and the wall next to it was beginning to crumble. The defenders of Acre knew that they were defeated. On 12 July 1191 they surrendered Acre in return for the lives of the Muslims in the city.

Dreadful decisions

As the defeated Muslims marched out of Acre, Richard's and Philip's banners were raised above the walls and towers of the devastated city. The two monarchs divided the property of Acre equally, but tension soon resurfaced because each king supported a different claimant to the throne of Jerusalem. Philip was allied to Conrad of Montferrat while Richard supported Guy of Lusignan. At the end of July it was agreed that Guy should hold the throne for his lifetime, but that on his death the crown should pass to his rival. By that time Philip had already made the decision to abandon the Third Crusade and return to France. Philip's continued ill health, his irritation at Richard's arrogance and the need to assert his rights over Flanders following the Count of Flanders' death at Acre, must all have influenced his decision. Before he left the Holy Land Philip swore that he would not attack Richard's territory in France. The English King did not trust Philip to keep his promise and the threat of Philip's interference in Angevin territory became an increasing distraction for the Lionheart during the remainder of the Third Crusade.

Of more immediate concern to Richard was Saladin's reluctance to honour the surrender terms following the fall of Acre. Saladin failed to hand over the True Cross that he had held since Hattin and he was in no hurry to release Frankish prisoners or to pay ransom money. The Lionheart knew that he could not afford a delay if the Third Crusade was to succeed. On 19 August Richard made the decision to kill all the Muslim prisoners taken at Acre, apart from the most important who could be ransomed. The next day Richard's men marched 2700 Muslim prisoners out of the city, bound in ropes. In an area of open ground beyond the crusaders' tents they set upon the Muslims with their swords and murdered them in cold blood. Richard's message to Saladin was clear: this was the ruthless brutality that he was prepared to bring to the Holy War.

▽ Richard the Lionheart watching the execution of Muslim prisoners at Acre. Detail from a French miniature, 1490.

> ■ Remember to add more notes to your timeline and key issues. Make sure you are clear about the nature of the rivalry between Richard and Philip and its impact on the Third Crusade.

The March to Jaffa, August 1191

What next? This was the question in the front of Richard's mind following his victory at Acre. The Third Crusade had been launched to recover Jerusalem, but, in August of 1191, it was not certain that a direct assault on the Holy City was the English King's immediate goal. Richard decided to lead his men south on an 80-mile march to the port of Jaffa, Jerusalem's port. It may have been his intention to use Jaffa as a springboard for an attack on the Holy City. Alternatively, Richard may have been planning to launch an attack from Jaffa on the southern coastal city of Ascalon. This would have cut off Saladin's crucial military and trade link to and from Egypt. It is also possible that Richard had not yet decided on a firm plan and that he intended to make up his mind when he reached Jaffa.

The Lionheart's immediate concern was to prize his men out of Acre. Many of the crusaders were enjoying the city's wine and women and were reluctant to set out on another military campaign. By 22 August, Richard had gathered around 15,000 of his troops, ordering that only elderly washerwomen were to accompany his men on their march south. At first there were some problems with organisation and discipline, but, after the first few days, Richard organised his army in a strict formation. As you can see on the diagram, the elite knights of the Templars and Hospitallers were positioned at the front and rear. The King and his mounted knights were in the middle. There could be no possibility of an attack from the right because Richard's men stuck close to the shoreline. On their left the King and his knights were protected by ranks of well-armed infantry. Richard further demonstrated his military leadership by ordering the crusaders' ships to sail down the coast with the army. Richard's navy would keep the crusaders supplied with food and weapons during their march along the coast.

The crusaders endured terrible conditions on their way to Jaffa. The summer heat was stifling and Saladin's forces placed them under near-constant attack. Six years after the events, the chronicler Ambroise wrote a vivid eyewitness account of the march. He described how Saladin's skilled horsemen made lightning strikes on the crusaders, showering the men and their horses with arrows and cross-bow bolts: 'never did the rain or

▽ **The March to Jaffa. The inset shows the formation of Richard's army on the march.**

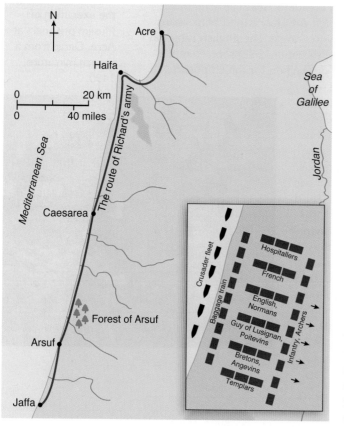

snow, or hail falling in the heart of winter fall so densely as did the bolts which flew and killed our horses'. The need to wear full armour meant that many men developed sunstroke and had to be evacuated to the ships. Richard's military leadership was crucial to the survival of the crusaders. He allowed the soldiers rest days and prevented fights over the meat of dead horses. He was particularly insistent that that no crusader should break rank and give chase to a Muslim horseman as he knew that the crusading army would be more vulnerable to attack if it broke formation.

The Battle of Arsuf, 7 September 1191

By 7 September, the crusaders were just 25 miles from Jaffa. Saladin was determined to stop them. If Richard's forces captured Jaffa so soon after the fall of Acre the consequences would be horrendous. The Muslims' hold over southern Palestine would be threatened and Saladin's reputation as the defender of Islam would be seriously damaged. Saladin therefore planned a massive assault on Richard's forces.

Saladin ordered his whole force of 30,000 men to attack the crusaders when they emerged from the wooded hills onto the plain north of Jaffa. Around nine o'clock, when the first of the crusaders marched onto the plain they were shocked to see Saladin's army waiting for them. Wave after wave of Muslim mounted warriors attacked the marching crusading army. Through this terrible onslaught, King Richard's priority was to keep his army moving forward in formation. He knew that a break in the line could prove fatal. Imagine the King's horror when he looked back and saw that two knights had suddenly broken ranks and were chasing Saladin's horsemen. Hundreds of crusaders were now following the two knights. Without hesitation, Richard turned his whole army on the Muslims. In the chaotic battle that followed Richard's men fought off two fierce Muslim counter attacks and made renewed charges, eventually forcing Saladin's army to retreat.

Richard the Lionheart's overall leadership at the Battle of Arsuf has recently come under closer scrutiny from the historian Thomas Asbridge. Asbridge argues that modern historians have too readily followed Ambroise's account of the event. This presents Richard as the great hero who actively sought the confrontation with Saladin at Arsuf. Using a wider range of sources, including a letter written by Richard shortly after the battle, Asbridge argues that Richard I reacted to events and that the King himself saw the Battle of Arsuf as simply a response to one of the many attacks that the crusaders had faced on their march to Jaffa. If the significance of Richard's role at Arsuf has been exaggerated, there is no doubt that the success of the crusaders in reaching Jaffa marked a significant turning point in the Third Crusade. Saladin had not been totally defeated, but after Arsuf the morale of the Muslims was seriously sapped.

■ Add points to your timeline and make further notes on the key issues. If you haven't done so already, start your notes on the leadership of Saladin.

How important was Richard's leadership during this phase of the Third Crusade?

To Jerusalem

The first attempt to take Jerusalem, October 1191–January 1192

The crusaders had only been in Jaffa a few days when worrying news reached them from southern Palestine. In order to prevent the crusaders taking Ascalon, Saladin had made the agonising decision to sacrifice the city. His men had begun to pull down Ascalon's walls. Richard argued for an immediate attack on the port in order to threaten Saladin's communications with Egypt. However, a large number of nobles resisted – they were determined to make a direct assault on Jerusalem. Richard could not persuade them to save Ascalon. The Third Crusade stalled. The crusaders remained in Jaffa and strengthened its fortifications. Some were no doubt distracted by the boatloads of prostitutes who arrived from Acre. Saladin took the opportunity to destroy the networks of crusader castles and fortifications between Jaffa and Jerusalem.

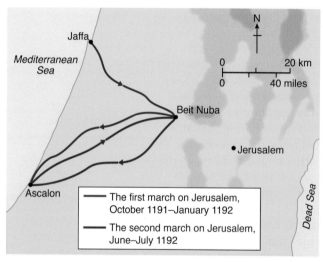

△ The marches on Jerusalem, 1191–92.

On 29 October 1191, the crusaders set out from Jaffa and began the painstaking work of rebuilding the crusader forts along the route to Jerusalem. They were repeatedly attacked by Saladin's troops. However, alongside these military skirmishes, the two sides were also engaged in diplomacy. A willingness to talk and to find areas of agreement, at the same time as engaging in brutal combat, was an important characteristic of the Third Crusade. Richard negotiated with the Sultan's brother, al-Adil and even offered his sister Joan to be one of al-Adil's wives as part of a deal to divide Palestine between the crusaders and the Muslims. Not surprisingly, Joan reacted rather badly to Richard's plan!

As winter set in, heavy rain and cold slowed down the crusaders. It took them nearly two months to reach Beit Nuba, twelve miles from Jerusalem. It was there that Richard, together with knights of the crusader states and the Military Orders, began to doubt the wisdom of laying siege to Jerusalem. They were worried that supply lines to the coast would be cut off by the Muslims and that, even if Jerusalem was taken, the crusaders would not have sufficient manpower to hold on to the Holy City. It was perhaps at this point that the impact of the death of Frederick Barbarossa and the departure of Philip II was felt most keenly. On 13 January, 1192, King Richard gave the order to withdraw. This was a devastating decision that shattered the morale of the Third Crusaders. Richard moved his increasingly depressed and divided army to Ascalon where he kept them busy rebuilding the walls of the city that Saladin had so recently torn down.

The second attempt to take to Jerusalem, June–July 1192

In the spring of 1192, Richard faced increasing pressures from both within and beyond the Holy Land. Divisions in the political leadership of the crusader states hardened when Conrad of Montferrat openly challenged the authority of Guy of Lusignan. The nobility began to turn against King Guy thinking that he would be unable to maintain the Kingdom of Jerusalem when the Crusade ended. In mid-April, Richard abandoned Guy and switched his support to Conrad. Then, in Tyre on 28 April, Conrad was stabbed to death by two assassins. Rumours began to spread that Richard had contracted the murder. The Lionheart's problems deepened when messengers arrived from Europe bringing news that his younger brother, Prince John, had exiled Richard's viceroy, William Longchamp, and had attempted a coup. On 29 May the King began to fear for his Angevin lands when he learned that Philip was plotting with John. Richard fell into a depression, unable to decide what to do next. On 31 May he was overtaken by events when the leading nobles of the Third Crusade decided to march on Jerusalem once more.

> A coup is an attempt to seize power.

When Saladin's spies brought him news of the renewed assault he immediately began to reassemble his armies. The Sultan was not in a strong position. Since his great victories at Hattin and Jerusalem in 1187, Saladin's commitment to jihad had deepened, but his capacity to fight the crusaders had weakened. The Sultan's financial resources were severely overstretched and he was struggling to pay for the on-going war. Saladin also faced potential divisions within the army and there were even signs of disloyalty within his own family. He had been fighting for six years and, for much of that time, had been debilitated by recurrent illness. In June 1192, Saladin's priority was to retreat to Jerusalem and to survive the Third Crusade.

This time the crusaders advanced on Jerusalem with much greater speed. By 10 June they had reached Beit Nuba. There they paused to await reinforcements and discuss strategy. Tipped off by local spies, the crusaders made a successful attack on a Muslim caravan taking supplies to Jerusalem. Morale was also boosted by the discovery of yet another piece of the True Cross. Many crusaders must have been aware of 15 July 1099 as the date when Jerusalem had fallen in the First Crusade. Inside the Holy City, Saladin began to despair. He ordered all the wells around Jerusalem to be poisoned and prepared to leave the city for his own safety. A Muslim chronicler later recorded that at Friday prayers on 3 July, Saladin's tears fell to his prayer rug in the Aqsa Mosque. But then, as evening fell, the Sultan received some astonishing news: the crusaders seemed to be in retreat!

There had been a heated debate in the crusader camp about whether a siege of Jerusalem could succeed. Richard argued that the vulnerability of the supply line back to Jaffa, the lack of water and Jerusalem's formidable defences made a successful attack unlikely. He was supported by the majority of the Crusade's leaders. Only the remaining French contingent wanted to continue. On 4 July the Third Crusade collapsed.

> ■ Make sure you keep adding notes to your timelines and issues documents. You should have plenty of ideas now about Saladin's leadership.

Truce

At the end of July 1192, Saladin decided to take advantage of the crusaders' retreat from Jerusalem by launching a lightning attack on Jaffa. In just four days the Muslim sappers and stone-throwers destroyed sections of Jaffa's walls. The small Christian garrison was forced to take refuge in the citadel of Jaffa. When King Richard heard of Jaffa's plight he rushed south from Acre at the head of a sea-borne counter attack. As they approached Jaffa the crusaders' boats stopped, unsure whether Saladin's forces had taken the citadel. One of the defenders managed to escape and swam to the Christian fleet, explaining that if they acted quickly there was still time to save the town. Richard knew that his men were heavily outnumbered, but he ordered them to attack and was one of the first to wade ashore at the head of his small army. The surprise of his attack gave the crusaders an improbable and dramatic victory. Richard's forces may have been unable to take Jerusalem, but his victory at Jaffa demonstrated his skill and valour as a military leader. It also showed that Saladin was incapable of driving the crusaders out of southern Palestine. Negotiation was now the only option.

Following his victory at Jaffa, Richard's energy was sapped and he fell dangerously ill. He was increasingly worried that his territories in France were in danger from the conspiracy between his brother John and Philip II. The time had come to sign a truce with Saladin. The Treaty of Jaffa was agreed on 2 September. In return for a three-year truce, Palestine was to be partitioned:

1   Saladin was to retain control of Jerusalem.

2   Ascalon's fortifications were once again to be destroyed.

3   The crusaders were allowed to keep the conquests of Acre and Jaffa, and the coastal strip between the two towns.

4   Christian pilgrims were allowed access to the Church of the Holy Sepulchre in Jerusalem.

In the month after the Treaty of Jaffa was signed, three groups of crusaders made their way to Jerusalem to visit the Holy Sepulchre. Richard was not among them. Maybe he was too ill or perhaps he could not bear to visit the Holy City while it was still held by the Muslims. His refusal to visit Jerusalem meant that he never met Saladin, apart from in the legends and pictures (such as the one we began with) which were created in the years following the Third Crusade.

■ Concluding your enquiry

So, what makes a good historical question about the Third Crusade? Think carefully about each of the following enquiry questions in relation to your annotated timeline and your notes on the key issues. In your opinion:

- Are any of these enquiry questions not worth asking?
- Which of the enquiry questions focus on the same issue, but from a different perspective?
- Which enquiry questions require most knowledge of the Third Crusade?
- Which of these enquiry questions would you be able to answer most confidently?
- Which is the best enquiry question about the Third Crusade?

1　Why did the Third Crusade end in stalemate?

2　Was the rivalry between Richard I and Philip II the main reason for the limited success of the Third Crusade?

3　Was Richard I a bad crusader?

4　Was the Battle of Arsuf the most important turning point in the Third Crusade?

5　Why did Richard I fail to recapture Jerusalem?

6　How far did western European politics determine the outcome of the Third Crusade?

7　Why was Saladin unable to defeat the Franks during the Third Crusade?

8　What were the achievements of Richard I on the Third Crusade?

9　How successful was the Third Crusade?

10　Does Richard I deserve to be remembered as a great crusader?

What happened to Saladin?

In the autumn of 1192 Saladin disbanded his armies. After touring his territories in Palestine, he returned to Syria and spent a rainy winter in Damascus. Early in 1193, Saladin's exhausted body began to give up on him. He developed a fever and sickness. His condition deteriorated and he began to slip in and out of consciousness. On 3 March 1193, Saladin died. He was 55. His body was interred in a mausoleum at the Grand Umayyad Mosque in Damascus where it remains to this day.

... and Richard I?

Richard sailed from Acre on 9 October and travelled through Europe in disguise in order to evade his enemies. In Vienna he was recognised and was imprisoned by Duke Leopold of Austria in the dungeons of a castle overlooking the River Danube. Richard was released in February 1194 on payment of a huge ransom. In April 1194, Richard was re-crowned in Winchester cathedral. He spent much of the next five years trying to recover the lands in Normandy taken by King Philip. While besieging a castle in southern France, Richard was struck in the shoulder by a crossbow bolt. The wound turned gangrenous and, on 6 April 1199, Richard died. He was 41. His body was buried at Fontevraud and his heart was interred at Rouen.

Remembering Richard I and Saladin

Richard I and Saladin are long dead, but the two men are firmly fixed in popular memory. In the middle of the nineteenth century Richard was represented in sculpture as a national hero. This was a period of growing nationalism and imperialism in Europe. It was also a time of romanticism when people looked back at the Middle Ages for inspiration. It's perhaps not surprising that Richard I was immortalised in stone as a great English hero. In the twentieth century the growth of Arab nationalism meant that Saladin, too, was remembered in stone. This insight into the statues of Richard and Saladin in London and Damascus reveals some interesting parallels in the ways in which the two leaders were portrayed.

In 1851, the Italian artist Carlo Marochetti was commissioned to make a plaster cast of Richard I for the Great Exhibition in London. The larger than life-size sculpture was the first thing that visitors saw as they approached the western entrance to the exhibition. Following the exhibition, the statue was moved to a position in front of the Houses of Parliament. Funds were raised for a bronze replica of the statue with Queen Victoria contributing £200. The statue was completed in 1860; it has stood in this prime position ever since, despite the fact that some people think it is no longer an appropriate symbol for such a sensitive location.

Marochetti portrayed Richard as a majestic warrior. The King makes a powerful figure, sitting proudly on his horse and brandishing his sword. When the statue was unveiled in 1860, some people noted Marochetti's artistic license in depicting Richard wearing close-fitting chain mail to show off his muscles, but the statue was generally admired. Marochetti

△ Carlo Marochetti's statue of Richard in front of the Houses of Parliament in London.

later added bronze scenes on the side of the granite plinth. These showed Richard in battle and on his deathbed. In the deathbed scene he is forgiving the French archer who shot him.

△ Abdallah al-Sayed's statue of Saladin in front of the citadel in Damascus.

This larger than life-size sculpture of Saladin was commissioned by President Hafiz al-Asad of Syria in 1992. Asad, who ruled Syria between 1971 and 2000, saw himself as a defender of Islam against western imperial powers and wanted others to see him as a twentieth-century Saladin. In Muslim countries it is rare to find sculptures depicting scenes from history so this makes the statue all the more remarkable. The statue was placed in front of the medieval citadel, one of the most important buildings in Damascus. Less than a hundred metres away, a massive portrait of Asad hung above the gate of the citadel.

In his sculpture, Abdallah al-Sayed depicted Saladin as a proud, mounted warrior urging his horse forward in combat with the crusaders. Saladin is flanked on one side by a soldier with his sword at the ready, and on the other by a Sufi holy man. To the rear of the horse al-Sayed has included the scene following the Battle of Hattin. King Guy of Jerusalem holds a bag of money containing his ransom. Reynald de Châtillon, whose life will not be spared, slumps against a rock and looks to the ground.

8 Who wrecked the Fourth Crusade?

▷ Pope Innocent III from a fresco on the wall of a monastery that he founded in Italy in 1203. The face captures his relative youthfulness and forceful determination.

On 8 January 1198, six years after the end of the Third Crusade, a new leader took charge of the Latin Church as Pope Innocent III. He was sure that God had called him to recapture Jerusalem. He quickly proclaimed a crusade to take the holy city and place it under Christian control for ever.

But intentions and outcomes can be very different.

In April 1204 Innocent's crusading force did capture one of the great cities of the world – but it was not Jerusalem and the enemy were not Muslims. It was Constantinople, the Christian capital city of the Byzantine Empire. Western Christians slaughtered eastern Christians, stealing their treasures and dismantling their empire. When the details of the fighting and looting reached Pope Innocent, he was appalled. The Crusade was officially abandoned. It never reached the Holy Land and the bitterness it caused between the Church in the east and the west lingers to this day.

■ **Enquiry Focus:** Who wrecked the Fourth Crusade?

In this enquiry we will take you through the extraordinary story of the Fourth Crusade and prompt you at regular intervals to consider how several key players can be held responsible for its failure. They are:

- Pope Innocent III, who called for the Crusade
- the lords, who planned the Crusade
- the Doge of Venice, who diverted the Crusade
- the Byzantine Prince Alexios, who promised to support the Crusade.

Preparation: the case against Innocent III

Earlier crusades responded to appeals for help from Christians in the east. On this occasion the Franks in the crusader states would have preferred not to provoke any further war. After the Treaty of Jaffa in 1192 Acre became the main city in the so-called Kingdom of Jerusalem. Saladin and his heirs ruled the holy city itself and allowed Christians to visit, but this was not enough for Pope Innocent. In August 1198, following a temporary breakdown in the truce, he issued his call for a new crusade.

Innocent called his crusade plans 'the business of the cross'. He adopted a business-like approach to identifying problems that might weaken the Crusade. Many of these problems had grown up over the previous century and other Popes had tried to tackle them, but Innocent believed his systematic response would help raise the most powerful crusading force yet seen. His mistake was in believing that strengthening papal control of the Crusade would deepen religious commitment and guarantee success.

Here are some of the changes he made:

- He discouraged half-hearted and inappropriate recruits by insisting that crusaders must serve for two years in the east.

- Relying on individuals to pay their own costs stopped some from crusading so Innocent introduced a church income tax to help pay the costs for poorer crusaders or to hire mercenaries. The tax took one fortieth of all church income. Lords and knights still paid their own way.

- He encouraged extra donations by offering indulgences to people who would finance someone else to join the Crusade on their behalf. Donors could now ease their way to heaven without needing to leave home and fight.

- The papacy appointed officially approved preachers to spread the message of the new crusade. In the past uncontrolled preaching had led to an over-enthusiastic mass response of poor unarmed pilgrims.

In the autumn of 1198 Pope Innocent sent his officially approved preachers to call people to crusade. In letters to church leaders he set out the changes shown above, expecting the new arrangements to bring a flood of suitable recruits. But the response was slow. There was no rush to join the Crusade and clergy were reluctant to pay the new tax.

Like all other Popes, Innocent relied on volunteers. Unfortunately two great sea powers, Genoa and Pisa, were at war and could not help transport crusaders by sea. Richard I of England and Philip II of France were also at war with each other. In late 1198 Innocent sent a papal legate to try to persuade these warring kings to make a truce so that they or at least their leading lords could join the new crusade. They both refused. Innocent did not target German lands as the papacy was once again in dispute with the German Emperor. When he wrote to the Byzantine Emperor seeking support for the Crusade, Innocent's high-handed tone once again drew an immediate refusal. In the end no kings took part, which deprived the Crusade of national taxation.

> See page 116 for the Treaty of Jaffa. It kept the peace quite steadily even after Saladin's death in 1193.

> For examples of problems with recruitment and military inefficiency in earlier crusades see pages 34, 76, 80, 82, 106 and 112.

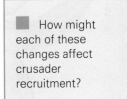
How might each of these changes affect crusader recruitment?

> Richard believed that the Pope was trying to order him to take part and was so insulted that he threatened to have the legate castrated.

The code of chivalry

To make matters worse, Innocent failed to grasp the priorities of the men he most needed to attract. Where their forefathers might have joined a crusade for personal spiritual reward in the form of an indulgence, lords and knights at the start of the thirteenth century were also motivated by the culture of chivalry. This stressed notions of courage, duty, honour and service. The knight's service was to his feudal lord rather than directly to the Church. One expression of this emerging culture came through organised tournaments in which the knights showed their prowess in mock battles and in face-to-face combat. The Church disapproved of the pride and violence of tournaments, but they were enormously popular.

It was in November 1199 at a great tournament at Écry in northern France that the breakthrough in crusade recruitment came. Later accounts claimed credit for the Pope by saying that one of Innocent's official preachers, Fulk of Neuilly, preached at the tournament, but there is no solid evidence that he was even at the event. In fact, it was probably the death of Richard I in March 1199 that made the difference. The lords who took the cross at Écry included Thibaut of Champagne and Louis of Blois who had been loyal to Richard but disliked and mistrusted his successor, King John. Going on crusade gave them an honourable way of avoiding fighting for John against King Philip of France. Louis, Thibaut and their friend Baldwin of Flanders, who also took the cross, came from families and regions with a strong tradition of crusading and others soon followed. But there is no evidence that any of these nobles felt any particular duty or service to Innocent III. They knew that his blessing of the Crusade offered spiritual rewards but they felt no special loyalty to him and certainly did not see him as the controller of the expedition.

▽ A crusader knight from a thirteenth-century psalter.

■ Start your summary of the 'Case against Innocent III'. Find evidence to support and develop the outline statements shown below.

- Innocent had no particular cause to call the Crusade in the first place and in many ways his timing was poor.
- Innocent's attempts to assert papal authority hindered recruitment rather than helped it. (The Crusade never recovered from weak recruitment.)

Planning: the case against the lords

In the spring of 1200, Count Thibaut of Champagne, Count Louis of Blois and Count Baldwin of Flanders started planning the Crusade, but made no attempt to co-ordinate their efforts with Pope Innocent. Their main decision was to travel by sea. This would be expensive but quick. It would also avoid having to cross the Byzantine Empire or deal with the Emperor. Most western Europeans thought the Byzantines were devious, believing that they failed to support the Franks at Antioch in the First Crusade and slowed the advance of German crusaders over their lands in the Third Crusade. Trade continued between the two halves of Christendom, but there remained an undercurrent of mutual mistrust.

There was also a hidden dimension to the decision to travel by sea: the nobles agreed secretly that the Crusade would not sail directly to the Levant, but that it would attack Egypt instead. Egypt's enormous wealth was certainly an attraction, but it was also the real centre of Muslim power and it had to be defeated if Jerusalem was to be taken. It was a sensible strategy, but they chose to let the mass of crusaders believe they would be sailing straight to the Holy Land, possibly because this would encourage recruitment. Even the Pope was not allowed to know that Egypt was the target for the Crusade.

The deal with Venice

The decision to travel by sea required the involvement of at least one of three Italian city states whose sea trade with the east had grown considerably over the twelfth century. The only realistic choice was Venice, as Genoa and Pisa were at war. One of the envoys was Geoffrey of Villehardouin, a knight who later wrote a history of the Fourth Crusade. By March 1201 Villehardouin and the other envoys were engaged in detailed planning with the Doge (ruler) of Venice, Enrico Dandolo. The Doge was an extraordinary man: he was over 90 years old and had been blind for many years, but was famous for his sharp mind, political skills and total commitment to the city of Venice.

To travel from one port required careful, co-ordinated planning. Everyone would need to arrive at Venice within a short space of time; all the ships and supplies would have to be ready; and the funds would have to be in place to pay the Venetians before the Crusade could get under way. This meant that the envoys sent by the lords had to tell the Doge how many crusaders there would be. All this proved too much for the leadership. They had no authority to bind any but their own followers to the agreement to sail from Venice. If they had worked with the Pope, it is just possible that a common agreement might have been made, but they had no way to predict the number who would sail from Venice. It seems they left it to the envoys to come up with an estimate. Villeharduoin and his colleagues told the Venetians to prepare to transport 33,500 men with horses, equipment and food supplies. This was a fatal miscalculation.

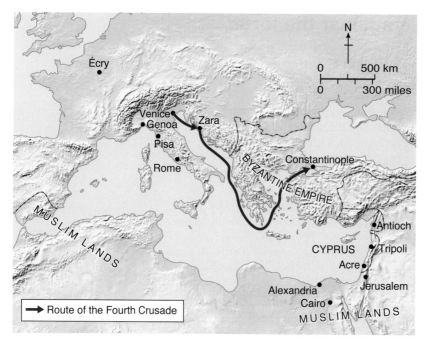

The price for transporting this enormous force was set by the Doge at 85,000 marks and half of whatever property was taken during the Crusade. This was a huge sum, but it was in keeping with the payments made to the Genoese by King Philip in the Third Crusade. This plan required Venice to limit its regular trading for a full year as it prepared and carried out the campaign, so the cost of the lost trade had to be met by the crusaders. The Doge gathered the people of Venice to St Mark's Cathedral and put the

△ **Europe and the Near East in 1204.**

proposal to them. His speech blended the enormous commercial benefits of establishing full Christian control of the Levant with the religious duty to support the Crusade. It met with enthusiastic support and the deal was confirmed. Only at this point were the treaty and estimated numbers and cost sent to Pope Innocent. He grudgingly agreed to the deal, alarmed at his lack of control over events.

Crisis point

When the crusaders gathered at Venice from June 1202 onwards, it became obvious that far fewer had taken the cross than had been expected and that not all of these were coming to Venice. Groups of crusaders had made their own way directly to Acre as they knew nothing of the plan to attack Egypt. Another reason for the low numbers may have been the death in May 1201 of Count Thibaut of Champagne, which deprived the Crusade of its most effective leader and of the thousands of knights and hired soldiers he would have brought with him. The remaining lords invited an Italian, Count Boniface of Montferrat, to join the Crusade as its leader. He was wealthy, respected and came from another strong crusading family, but he did not fit easily into the leading group, being an Italian and older than the French lords. Nor did he bring as many men as Thibaut might have done … and even these arrived late. In the end only 13,000 of the anticipated 33,500 crusaders turned up. This meant that the army was weaker than expected and, worst of all, the reduced number had nowhere near enough money to pay the Venetians who had prepared a fleet and provisions for the full total and expected to be paid accordingly. The Pope's tax on clergy had not raised anywhere near the sum he had hoped for and, besides, it was never intended to pay for a deal made privately by the French lords. The Crusade was already in crisis.

■ Start your summary of the 'Case against the nobles'. Find evidence to support and develop the outline statements shown below.

- The lords failed to liaise with Pope Innocent III.
- The lords entered agreements with Venice that were simply foolish.

Add extra evidence to your 'Case against Innocent III' if you can.

Diversion: the case against Enrico Dandolo

Problem and proposal

In August 1202 the Crusade was, quite literally, going nowhere. Thirteen thousand crusaders were camped on an island just outside Venice. Their leaders could not pay the Venetians for the fleet of ships that lay ready in the harbour. The Doge refused to let the crusaders leave without paying their debt and threatened to cut their supplies of food and drink. Even if they had been allowed home, the crusaders would have faced ridicule. For his part, the Doge would be remembered as the leader who lost his city a fortune by his reckless deal. The deadlock seemed complete.

But the Doge proposed a way forward. In September 1202, he offered to postpone payment by the crusaders and to sail them to Egypt as originally agreed if they would first fight on behalf of Venice against its local rivals from the city of Zara in Croatia. This city had recently broken away from Venetian control. If the crusaders accepted his deal, Venice would regain a valuable asset, he would save face by serving the best interests of his beloved city and the Crusade could continue. This mattered to him. If Venice could help conquer Egypt, it would gain Alexandria, the richest trading port in the Mediterranean. He also longed to follow his father and grandfather who had both fought in a crusade in 1122. He, like them, saw no contradiction between gaining riches and winning the spiritual rewards of a crusade indulgence. As an old man he was as eager as anyone to ensure the salvation of his soul. With this in mind, and to ensure he could influence the Crusade's leadership, he took the cross himself. Thousands of Venetians then followed his lead.

The deal seemed perfect but there was one very important problem: the people of Zara were Christians and their lord, the King of Hungary, had sworn the crusader oath himself. If they were to attack the Zarans, this Crusade would be waging war against fellow Christians for the commercial benefit of Venice. The Doge explained that the King of Hungary had taken his crusader vow over a year before and showed no sign of actually joining a crusade. He also insisted that Zara belonged to Venice anyhow.

Diversion and division

The leaders accepted the Doge's plan. It seemed the only way to continue the Crusade. In an emotional ceremony in the cathedral, the Doge took the cross. Thousands of Venetians followed his lead and, in a grand spectacle, the crusader fleet left Venice at last in October 1202, although the leaders had not yet told the rank and file crusaders where they were headed. By this time Pope Innocent had learned of the plan and told his legate at Venice to forbid the attack on Zara. The legate decided to wait until just before the attack was due to happen. But the Doge guessed what he would do and cleverly banned him from sailing with the fleet. The Pope had lost his voice among the Crusade leadership.

In November the crusaders arrived at Zara. When their leaders told them they were to attack this Christian city many refused to take part in the action. The Doge's plan was splitting the crusader army. But Zara quickly fell to the remaining crusaders in late 1202 and was returned to Venetian control. Pope Innocent was furious and **excommunicated** all the

■ Find evidence to support and develop the outline statement shown below.

• Enrico Dandolo diverted the Crusade for the material benefit of the city of Venice.

Add extra evidence to the other cases you have prepared so far.

crusaders. The French soon repented and Innocent made them swear to continue the Crusade with no further attacks on Christian lands 'without just or necessary cause'. But the Doge and Venetians felt they had done nothing wrong. They refused to take the oath.

Destruction: the case against Prince Alexios

At the end of December 1202 the crusaders were still camped at Zara when they received a message from Prince Alexios of Byzantium, the son of the former Byzantine Emperor, Isaac II. In 1195 Isaac had been forced to give up his throne by his brother who became Alexios III. Isaac had been blinded and thrown into prison in Constantinople, but Prince Alexios escaped and set about visiting European rulers hoping to gain their help in restoring Isaac to the throne. When he learned that the Crusade had financial problems Prince Alexios put together a proposal: if the crusaders would use their army to restore his father to the Byzantine throne, he promised them two remarkably generous rewards:

1   He would place the whole Byzantine Empire under the spiritual authority of the Pope, ending all conflict between Greek and Latin Churches.

2   He would pay 200,000 silver marks and provide 10,000 highly trained men to join the Crusade, making it a formidable force.

These terms would wipe out any remaining Venetian debts, re-unify Christendom under Pope Innocent III and allow the Crusade to the Holy Land to continue, with added strength, after a diversion to Constantinople. The Doge was particularly keen to accept as he knew Venice would gain long-term trading privileges with Constantinople if the plan went well. But Christian crusaders would be attacking another Christian city to depose a Christian ruler, Alexios III. This would break the oath that Innocent had made the crusaders swear after attacking Zara. The message from Prince Alexios reminded the leaders that Alexios III had taken the throne from Isaac II by force and insisted that it was their Christian duty to restore Isaac, conveniently ignoring the fact that Isaac had murdered his own way to the throne in 1185. Alexios also assured the Crusade's leaders that the Byzantine people would quickly take his side when he returned to Constantinople: no serious fighting would be needed. The deal was done.

The decision to make war on fellow Christians in Constantinople was too much for a good number of crusaders who left the official expedition in spring 1203. The Pope sent a letter telling the crusaders not to interfere in Byzantine affairs, but by June, when he sent it, the main crusader fleet, now with Prince Alexios himself on board, was just reaching Constantinople. Almost immediately it became obvious that young Alexios had either been highly optimistic or deeply deceptive about the welcome they would receive. When he appeared on deck as his ship sailed close to the massive walls of the city, the inhabitants ignored him. It was clear that Alexios III would not surrender his throne. A serious battle lay ahead.

Many of the crusaders who left the expedition in 1203 made their own way to the Holy Land but achieved very little when they arrived.

The rise of Prince Alexios

On 3 July, after much prayer, the crusaders landed on the shores of Constantinople and, thanks to the poor tactics of Alexios III and a half-hearted defence by his Byzantine forces, they established a foothold outside the city. This pattern was repeated over the next two weeks. At one point the aged, blind Doge insisted on being carried ashore at the head of an attack to inspire his men to victory. On the night of 17 July Alexios III fled from the city. The court officials released Isaac II from prison and asked him to rule the empire once more, this time as co-emperor with Prince Alexios. The crusaders expected their rewards.

Within weeks it was obvious that the Prince (now Alexios IV) could not honour the promises he had made to the crusaders: his father Isaac and Church leaders disapproved of the terms he had offered and dragged their feet over the promise to submit the eastern Church to rule from Rome. Alexios started to pay the silver and gold he had promised by melting down ancient church treasures which upset his own people. Matters were made worse when an outbreak of violence between locals and crusaders caused a fire that inflicted immense damage on Constantinople. Neither Alexios nor the crusaders should have been surprised at any of this. Even the rare partnerships between western Europe and the Byzantine Empire in the First and Second Crusades were very tentative. Despite regular trade between the two, most Byzantines saw the westerners as crude, greedy and bent on the conquest of their Empire. They could point to Bohemund's attempts to invade Anatolia in 1107, the Venetian attack on Corfu during their crusade of 1122, the capture of Corfu by Roger of Sicily during the Second Crusade and Richard I's conquest of Cyprus in the Third Crusade. There were anti-western riots in Constantinople in 1171 and again in 1182. After each of these, relationships were restored and trade continued but the undercurrents were negative.

The fall of Prince Alexios

Matters came to a head in November 1203 when Alexios stopped paying the cash he had promised. When reminded of the agreement he had made, Alexios felt his honour was being questioned and insulted the Doge, who was furious and swore to crush the young Emperor. It was clear to the court at Constantinople that Isaac II and Alexios had lost control and a Byzantine nobleman seized power. In January 1204 he took the throne as Alexios V, murdering both Prince Alexios and Isaac II. The crusaders faced a desperate crisis. They needed to spend the winter in their camp outside Constantinople before they could sail for Egypt but the new Emperor had killed their original protector and now refused to feed them. The leaders decided that their only hope of surviving and continuing the Crusade lay in taking Constantinople under their own control.

In April 1204, the crusaders sailed specially adapted Venetian ships up to the defences of Constantinople landing troops at, or even on, its mighty walls. Once they broke through, Alexios V fled and the leading Byzantine courtiers announced the city's surrender. If they hoped to avoid further violence, they were sadly disappointed.

Byzantine Emperors 1185–1204

1185: Isaac II, until deposed by his brother who became …

1195: Alexios III, until crusaders removed him and installed …

1203: Isaac II (again) and Alexios IV (Prince Alexios), until they were murdered by the noble who took over as …

1204: Alexios V … until the crusaders removed him and took over the city (see page 128).

The city's surrender signalled a devastating three-day wave of destruction and looting by the crusaders. They had sworn before the attack to respect the citizens, but householders were beaten and women were raped. They had also agreed in advance that all their booty would be pooled so that it could be used to pay off the remaining debts to the Venetians before sharing the rest between them. In fact this encouraged them to take even more, keeping some for themselves. Religious treasures were especially prized and one western abbot was seen with his robes bulging with precious books, vessels and holy relics. Beneath the dome of Haghia Sofia, the most magnificent church in the world, a prostitute danced on the altar as donkeys carried away its wealth on their backs.

Romania – a new crusader state to defend

Having conquered the city, the crusaders crowned Baldwin of Flanders as the ruler of a new Latin empire of Constantinople on 16 May 1204. This new empire, sometimes called Romania, was made up of the Byzantine lands in Europe, with different parts being ruled by the leading crusaders. The Venetians took the islands of Crete and Corfu which, with their control of all the trade that flowed through Constantinople, hugely added to their own city's wealth. To this day, a treasury in Venice is filled with beautiful Byzantine works of art taken there from Constantinople after 1204. The Doge sent many treasures home, including four ancient bronze horses that were placed high above the entrance to the great cathedral of San Marco in Venice as a symbol of triumph. He never returned to Venice, though, as he died in Constantinople in June 1205, still under excommunication.

At first Pope Innocent was pleased to hear that much of the old Byzantine Empire was now under papal authority, but his reaction changed to fury and shame when detailed reports reached him of the death, destruction, rape, and pillage that the crusaders had inflicted on Constantinople. As for the Crusade, it was decided in 1205 to abandon the campaign so that Romania could be secured. Some crusaders stayed to defend it from rebellions by Greeks and invasions by pagan tribes, but most returned home. They had not faced a single Muslim enemy in battle.

▽ San Marco cathedral in Venice. The horses just visible above the main entrance are copies of those sent to Venice from Constantinople by the Doge in 1204. The cathedral has an astonishing treasury, still filled with works of art taken from Byzantine churches.

- Find evidence to support the outline statement shown below.
- Without Prince Alexios the Crusade would never have gone to Constantinople. Once there, it was his weakness that led to the sacking of the city in 1204.

Add extra evidence to the other cases you have prepared so far.

■ Concluding your enquiry

As you were constructing the case against each person or group in this enquiry, you may have found it strange to be so one-sided. Now go back over each case and prepare a case for that person or group's defence. You will be able to use other parts of the story to show that their actions can be defended when understood in a wider context.

Finally, having considered both sides, decide who – if anyone – seems to have been most responsible for wrecking the Fourth Crusade.

Postscript – the story after 1204

The disastrous diversion of the Fourth Crusade did not end the West's attempts to reclaim Jerusalem, but the pattern of more or less constant failure that had been set since 1099 continued into the thirteenth century.

The Fifth Crusade (1217–21) From 1213 a massive preaching and fund-raising campaign supported a series of expeditions. In the main campaign, a crusader army landed in Egypt in 1219 but was defeated by the Egyptians in 1221.

The Sixth Crusade (1227–29) In this expedition, Frederick II of Germany achieved some success through diplomacy. He negotiated the surrender of Jerusalem to the Christians by allowing Muslims to control their own sacred sites in the city. But the deal ended in 1244. From then until 1917 Muslims ruled Jerusalem.

The Seventh Crusade (1248–54) This was an exceptionally well-planned, well-funded campaign led by the saintly King Louis IX of France ... and it was a complete failure. The crusaders landed in Egypt but were destroyed by the Muslim armies and by disease. Years later, when the crusader states faced destruction, King Louis launched ...

The Eighth Crusade (1268–70) In the late 1250s a powerful military group called the **Mamluks** rose to power in Egypt. In 1260 these Mamluks defeated an invading army from Asia, the Mongols. Until then these Mongols had been unstoppable, sweeping through central Asia, Iraq and Syria. An army that could defeat the mighty Mongols was sure to turn on the feeble crusader states. And it did. In 1268 the Mamluk leader, Baibars, marched his army against the city of Antioch taking it in a single day and massacring its entire people. King Louis IX crossed the Mediterranean aiming to crush the Mamluks in Egypt but on the way he fell ill and died in 1270. His army returned home.

The Ninth Crusade (1271–72) Lord Edward, the son of King Henry III of England, sailed to Acre to defend it from Baibars. He won a ten-year truce between the Franks and the Mamluks. In 1272, his father died and he returned to England to rule as King Edward I.

The end of the crusader states in the Near East (1291) After the ten-year truce had ended, the Mamluks set about wiping out the last remaining crusader cities. Tripoli fell in 1289 and then, in 1291, Acre was taken and destroyed. This time, no Europeans came to fight for the crusader states. The Muslims' victory was complete.

Insight

Crusader motivation – a historian's insight

This is the historian Jonathan Phillips, professor of Crusading History at Royal Holloway, University of London. He has written many books and articles and contributed to many broadcasts on the crusades. He has also acted as the historical consultant for this book.

In Holy Warriors, published in 2009, Jonathan wrote that '... the question of motivation shimmers and shifts across time and space, and trying to trace it is part of the challenge and excitement of this subject'. We wanted to know how his ideas on crusader motivation were developing so we asked him a few questions on a subject that clearly intrigues him. You can read his answers below. You should be able to detect not only what he thinks but how, as a professional historian, he has arrived at those conclusions and how interpretations change over time.

Q What motivated the crusaders?

A This is a question that motivates me! In one sense, we can never know what impelled individuals to act at this huge distance over time and space. But, as historians, we can try to gather as much evidence as possible and assess and evaluate this material to produce a reasonable answer. With regards to recent research on the motives of the earliest crusaders, the work of Riley-Smith and Bull during the 1990s, both of whom made extensive use of charter evidence, has done much to emphasise the centrality of religious devotion as a driving force behind the First Crusaders' actions. Charters have also enabled historians (Riley-Smith, Phillips) to identify family networks of crusaders, revealing that certain kin-groups were particularly consistent participants in these expeditions to the point where clear traditions evolved, thus forming another reason to take the cross.

See page 35 for information on charters.

Q How have your ideas evolved over the years?

A My recent work on Caffaro of Genoa, arguably the first secular historian of the crusades, has done much to influence my thinking and to make me look more widely at the issue of motive. Caffaro went to the Holy Land himself in 1101 and he later produced accounts of the Genoese actions there, as well as a text describing the capture of Almeria (1147) and Tortosa (1148) in Spain during the Second Crusade. A couple of lines from his writings were a starting point for me; he described the return of the 1101 fleet 'in triumph and covered in glory, as with the first Frankish army against Antioch in 1097, in the African expedition of 1087, in the first expedition to Tortosa [in Spain] in 1093 and when Jerusalem was taken in 1099.' This seemed to show a man for whom the campaigns in the Holy Land were part of a continuum of earlier conflicts with Muslim lands in Spain and North Africa. One reason for this was his perspective as an inhabitant of a Mediterranean trading city (Genoa).

Q Could seeking financial gain and striving for the glory of God work together?

A The Genoese had traded with the Muslim world for decades before the First Crusade; to cease doing so would have been economic suicide. Yet Genoa was filled with churches, reflecting conventional contemporary religiosity; it was also visited by preachers for the First Crusade in 1096. Men from Genoa took the cross and over the next few years a series of fleets sailed to the Holy Land where they offered crucial support during the early stages of the Frankish conquests. Frankish knights who settled in the Levant were rewarded with land, but the Genoese sought different economic advantages – trading privileges, judicial rights and areas of a city. This did not preclude religiously motivated behaviour because at the same time we see the Genoese taking relics back to their home city and participating in the customary activities of pilgrimage. The former group of settlers are barely criticised, but for the Genoese to seek more overt financial advancement seems to smack of the worldly motives so disdained by the ecclesiastical chroniclers of the day. The bottom line is, however, that without the Italian trading cities, the crusader states could not have functioned.

Q What does this teach us?

A The material from Genoa adds another dimension to the multi-faceted issue of crusade motivation. We should not forget that the Italian city-states (Genoa, Pisa and Venice) were prominent in the conquest of the Holy Land and that they were religiously, as well as commercially, driven. They continued to trade with various Muslim powers throughout the crusading period, although as the Islamic Near East became stronger under Nur ad-Din and Saladin, this would become increasingly difficult to justify.

We should not regard the First Crusaders as, to put it crudely, simply Frankish knights and their followers. Yes, this group was the dominant military force, but crusaders came from the Mediterranean world too and they brought with them a different and pre-existing set of relationships with Muslims (some positive, some not), and thus had another, and arguably more complex, range of reasons for taking the cross. The ecclesiastical chroniclers of (in many cases) northern Europe with whom we are so familiar emphasised – rightly – the religious motives of the crusaders. But we should allow for a further perspective as we try to understand why so many people across the Latin West became involved in the crusades. Caffaro regarded himself as a pious lay crusader from a booming trading city on the Mediterranean. This viewpoint is encapsulated in a Genoese document that described the capture of Almeria in 1147 as being 'to the glory of God, and of the whole of Christendom... [and] ... to the glory and profit of Genoa.'

Bibliography

Caffaro, *Genoa and the Twelfth Century Crusades*, trans. M.A. Hall and J.P. Phillips (Farnham, 2013)
See also:
M.G. Bull, *Knightly Piety and the Lay Response to the First Crusade* (Oxford, 1993)
J.P. Phillips, *Holy Warriors* (London, 2009)
J.P. Phillips, *The Second Crusade: Extending the Frontiers of Christendom* (London, 2007)
J.S.C. Riley-Smith, *The First Crusaders, 1095–1131* (Cambridge, 1997).

9 Does it matter what we think about the Crusades?

These England supporters are enjoying themselves with a beer before watching their football team play an international match abroad. They seem cheerful enough in their crusader outfits even if they are blissfully unaware of the fact that the crusaders were serial losers!

It is odd that England fans dress up as crusaders. After all, most crusaders were probably French, but might well have been from almost any part of Europe. If the fans are modelling themselves on a particular crusader, it might be 'Richard the Lionheart' (who spoke French not English and spent only seven months of his reign in England). They may even be confusing crusaders with St George (who was probably a Syrian soldier who lived long before the Crusades). To add to the confusion, the word 'crusade' in their mind may simply mean any campaign against a perceived injustice. Of course, the fans probably did not feel the need to research the facts, just fancy dress shops. If we were to point out their historical errors, they might tell us not to let the facts get in the way of a good story and ask us to share a beer with them. And, in this case, it probably doesn't matter that their interpretation is more myth than history. But there are times when confusing myth with historical fact is a far more serious matter, as we will see.

There is no activity for you in this final enquiry but, as you read, you might find it helpful to reflect on all the different influences at work in shaping our interpretations of history.

The popular view of crusading: from Walter Scott to Ridley Scott

We often carry ideas about the past in our heads without knowing how they got there. In this case, the football fans' assumptions about crusaders are probably rooted in stories that have been passed on since

Sir Walter Scott, the most successful popular novelist of his day, wrote *The Talisman* in 1825. The story unfolds in the romanticised setting of the Near East during the Third Crusade. Even though most crusaders in the story are greedy, crude and arrogant towards the Muslims, King Richard I is the model of a crusader king. Scott invents a crucial encounter between King Richard I and Saladin. Saladin admires Richard's enormous, two-handed sword. Richard displays the sword's quality, and his own strength, by cutting clean through an iron bar. Saladin then reaches for his own slim, razor-sharp scimitar, spreads a silk veil over its blade and, to the astonishment of all, by a simple, swift movement, he cuts it in two. The message was clear: each sword – and each culture – was remarkable in its own way. At its best, the Christian culture was direct, honest and strong, but there was something especially admirable in the subtlety and sophistication of Saladin's fine weapon and the culture of the Muslim world. The book fixed these ideas in the popular imagination, and they have remained there ever since.

This romanticised view of the Crusades continued through the Victorian era. In the middle of the twentieth century it was still found in children's books, such as the title shown on the right. Other books, television programmes and films since the mid-twentieth century have consistently told stories of Robin Hood, where King Richard's absence on the Crusades suggests nobility and virtue. The effect has been to create a popular image of crusaders at their best as men of honour, fighting for a just cause with simple, direct honesty and courage. But at their worst, as in Scott's novels, they are selfish, bigoted, brutes, blind to the sophistication of the Muslim culture they are attacking.

In 2004 the British director Sir Ridley Scott released details of a film he was working on, called *Kingdom of Heaven*. It was set in the years just before the capture of Jerusalem by Saladin in 1187. It contrasted the honourable conduct of the fictional hero with sadistic and villainous behaviour by the Knights Templar and the cowardly greed of the Christian clergy. Above all, it showed Saladin as a wise and merciful leader, punishing evil and respecting courage.

On hearing a summary of the plot, Jonathan Riley-Smith, a leading historian of the Crusades, commented that '… it sounds absolute balls. It's rubbish. It's not historically accurate at all. It draws on *The Talisman*, which depicts the Muslims as sophisticated and civilised and the crusaders are all brutes and barbarians'. He later added the view that the film was perpetuating an interpretation that could not be further from what Crusade historians now believe, but that any attempts by these historians to communicate their carefully researched ideas to wider society were like 'whispering into a gale'. The popular view is firmly fixed and far from that held by academic historians. But does it matter?

▽ Richard I on his white horse crushing Muslims beneath its feet. This image is from a children's history book published in England in 1937 called *A Pageant of Kings*. The title given to this picture was 'The Mighty King of Chivalry'.

A Muslim perspective: From Abu'l-Fida to Osama bin Laden

A fourteenth-century Muslim historian, Abu'l-Fida, ended his account of the expulsion of the Franks from the crusader states in 1291, by listing the lands they had once claimed and by praying 'God grant that they never set foot there again!' And for hundreds of years, they did not. During those centuries the Muslim world more or less forgot the Crusades as its own power reached far into Europe. A new tribe of Turks, the **Ottomans**, conquered Constantinople in 1453 and took control of much of south-east Europe. The time when the Christians had briefly held Jerusalem seemed of little importance compared with their own successes. The view changed, however, as the Ottoman Empire declined and western states once again took control of Muslim-held lands. This time the attacks, such as Britain's occupation of Egypt in 1882, were not launched by the Pope but by governments.

This new round of western conquests was part of a worldwide expansion of power that we now call colonialism. The colonialists of the nineteenth century believed they were spreading the benefits of western society to lands they regarded as uncivilised. In France the historian Joseph Michaud looked back to the Crusades and wrote about those medieval campaigns as if they had been fought with this same purpose. His *History of the Crusades* appeared in 1812 and remained popular for the rest of the century. Later editions were illustrated by impressive, romanticised engravings by Gustav Dore. The message of the book and the images was that France had brought light and law to the east by its leading role in the Crusades.

△ Gustav Dore's 1875 illustration of Godfrey of Bouillon entering Jerusalem in the First Crusade. He seems invincible and the light of civilisation follows him into the city.

In the 1890s, prompted by western colonialism, Arab scholars reawakened interest in the Crusades. They studied Michaud and decided that the West's invasion of Muslim lands, whether in the Middle Ages or in the more recent colonialism, was driven by greed and by a desire to destroy Islam. To them, the question of whether the Pope authorised the campaign and whether spiritual rewards were on offer did not matter: all these western attacks, over many centuries, were crusades.

By 1950 this interpretation seemed even more likely to be true from the perspective of Muslims. By then western powers had taken control of the old Ottoman Empire after the First World War and had set up the state of Israel on the same land that had once been the crusaders' Kingdom of Jerusalem. This felt like a continuation of the Crusades. The Scott–Michaud view of crusading matched their experience: the West was out to take Muslim land.

In the last years of the twentieth century, militant Muslims known as Islamists, were still convinced that the West wanted to take Muslim lands and destroy Islam. They decided to resist and called for jihad against the western powers. A Saudi Arabian Islamist, Osama bin Laden, set up the organisation known as al Qaeda to support violent resistance to what he called 'Global Crusaders'. Al Qaeda's most shocking attack struck the United States on '9/11' (11 September 2001). Bin Laden justified this as an act of resistance against the West's interference in Muslim lands.

A dangerous cocktail

The term 'crusade' has acquired all sorts of meanings. It may suggest:

- any campaign against a perceived injustice
- romanticised images of sophisticated Muslims defending their land against crude and bigoted knights
- heroic westerners fighting to spread Christian values
- a sinister, centuries old attempt by western powers to destroy Islam.

In recent years these various myths and misunderstandings have come together in a dangerous cocktail.

Just days after the devastating events of 9/11, George Bush, President of the United States, pledged that the people behind the attacks would be caught but cautioned that 'this crusade … this war on terror is going to take a while'. His aides quickly reassured the world that the President was using the word 'crusade' in the loose sense of a campaign, but ever since that statement bin Laden and other Islamists have used it as proof that the West is continuing a mission to destroy Islam that began over 900 years ago with the medieval crusaders.

In 2005, the film *Kingdom of Heaven* which showed most crusaders and churchmen in a bad light became very popular, particularly in the Arab world. This had been the fear of historian Jonathan Riley-Smith who had criticised the plot as the film was being made. He insisted that:

> … the fanaticism of most of the Christians in the film and their hatred of Islam is what the Islamists want to believe. At a time of inter-faith tension, nonsense like this will only reinforce existing myths.

Then, in July 2011 a Norwegian, Anders Breivik, murdered over 70 of his fellow citizens, claiming to be a 'modern-day crusader'. His victims included 69 young people who belonged to a political party that he believed allowed too many Muslims to come and live in Norway. Hours before this dreadful slaughter, Breivik circulated a manifesto on the internet in which he claimed to be some sort of Templar Knight carrying out a crusade to defend Europe from Muslim attack. His understanding of the Crusades was highly confused and based on uncritical use of the internet. His ignorance was deadly.

Does it matter what we think about the Crusades?

Yes!

▽ The cover of the manifesto of Anders Breivik. The date 2083 marks the 450th anniversary of the capture of Christian Constantinople by the Muslim Turks. Breivik aimed to drive all Muslims out of Europe by 2083.

2083

A European Declaration of Independance

Who? What? When? A summary of key events and people in this book

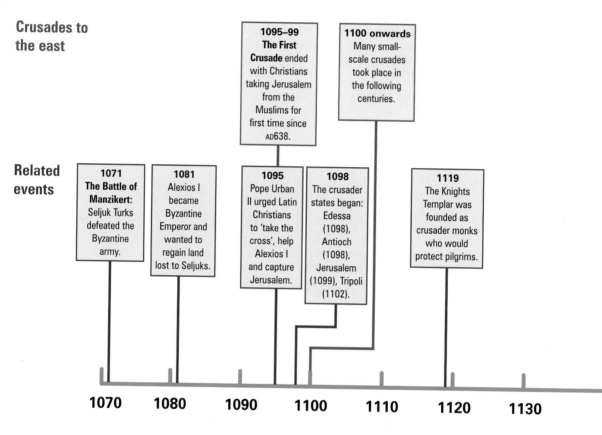

Crusades to the east

1095–99 The First Crusade ended with Christians taking Jerusalem from the Muslims for first time since AD638.

1100 onwards Many small-scale crusades took place in the following centuries.

Related events

1071 The Battle of Manzikert: Seljuk Turks defeated the Byzantine army.

1081 Alexios I became Byzantine Emperor and wanted to regain land lost to Seljuks.

1095 Pope Urban II urged Latin Christians to 'take the cross', help Alexios I and capture Jerusalem.

1098 The crusader states began: Edessa (1098), Antioch (1098), Jerusalem (1099), Tripoli (1102).

1119 The Knights Templar was founded as crusader monks who would protect pilgrims.

1070   1080   1090   1100   1110   1120   1130

People

Alp Arslan led the Seljuk Turks and de-stabilised Muslim/ Christian relations by taking Byzantine land.

Alexios I was prepared to ask for help from Latin Christians believing it would help restore Byzantine power.

Pope Urban II believed the Crusade would purify and unite Christians.

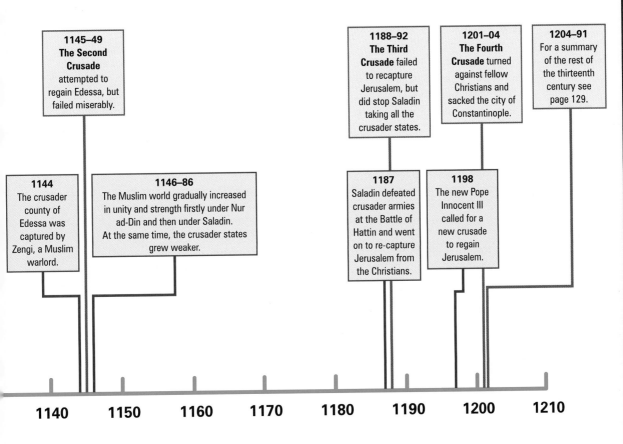

1145–49
The Second Crusade attempted to regain Edessa, but failed miserably.

1188–92
The Third Crusade failed to recapture Jerusalem, but did stop Saladin taking all the crusader states.

1201–04
The Fourth Crusade turned against fellow Christians and sacked the city of Constantinople.

1204–91
For a summary of the rest of the thirteenth century see page 129.

1144
The crusader county of Edessa was captured by Zengi, a Muslim warlord.

1146–86
The Muslim world gradually increased in unity and strength firstly under Nur ad-Din and then under Saladin. At the same time, the crusader states grew weaker.

1187
Saladin defeated crusader armies at the Battle of Hattin and went on to re-capture Jerusalem from the Christians.

1198
The new Pope Innocent III called for a new crusade to regain Jerusalem.

1140   1150   1160   1170   1180   1190   1200   1210

Zengi was the first Muslim to lead serious resistance to crusader kingdoms after years of Muslim disunity.

Louis VII of France and **Conrad III of Germany** were the leaders who returned to Europe in shame after the Second Crusade.

Nur ad-Din was the son of the warlord Zengi. He carried on his father's work in unifying Muslim lands in the Near East, often by conquest.

Saladin was a general who first served Nur ad-Din and then made himself leader of the Muslim Near East by 1185. In 1187 he recaptured Jerusalem from the crusaders.

Richard I of England and **Phillip II of France** led the Third Crusade but never overcame their personal rivalry.

Doge Enrico Dandolo of Venice was the aged joint-leader of the Fourth Crusade who fought for both wealth and religious salvation.

Glossary

Abbasids The family that ruled as caliphs of Islam between 750 and 1258. They followed Sunni Muslim traditions.

Anatolia The area of land that occupies most of modern Turkey, sometimes referred to as Asia Minor. (See the map on page 3.)

Armenia(n) Area of land to the south-east of the Black Sea. Armenians were Christians and they spread widely through the Near East.

Balkans The region in south-east Europe between Greece and the Black Sea. (See the map on page 3.)

Byzantine Empire The Greek-speaking eastern half of the Roman Empire. It survived long after the Roman Empire in the west collapsed in the fifth century. It was named after Byzantium, the capital city that was re-named as Constantinople in 330.

Caliph The title of the ruler of Islam after the death of the Prophet Muhammad. In theory there was only ever one caliph at a time, but as Islam split, different caliphs could be found, for example in Baghdad, Cairo and Spain.

Chivalry A code of behaviour adopted by medieval knights in western Europe.

Citadel A fortress.

Crusader states Lands in the Near East ruled by Christian Franks between 1099 and 1291. (See the map on page 50.)

Dome of the Rock A Muslim shrine built on the site in Jerusalem where Muslims believe the Prophet Muhammad was taken up to heaven to be taught by God how to pray.

Emir A high-ranking office in the Muslim world, similar to a prince.

Excommunicated To be excluded by the Pope from being a member of the Catholic Church and therefore unable to receive the sacraments necessary to reach heaven.

Fatimids The Muslim group that ruled north Africa and then Egypt between 909 and 1191. They claimed to be descendants of Fatima, the daughter of the Prophet Muhammad, and followed Shi'ah traditions.

Franks The name given to tribes who lived in northern Europe in the early Middle Ages. Muslims called all crusaders Franks or 'Franj'.

German Empire The large area of land that covered much of modern Germany, Austria, Switzerland, northern Italy and eastern France. Its different parts were ruled by many lords who all owed allegiance to an Emperor.

Greek Church The Church of the Byzantine Empire. Its forms of worship and its beliefs differed in many ways from the Latin Church of western Europe.

Greek fire Clay pots filled with flammable sulphur, resin and oils. On impact the pots exploded like bombs.

Hajj The pilgrimage (religious journey) made by Muslims to Makkah.

Haram al-Sharif The Arabic name for the Temple Mount in Jerusalem which was the site of the ancient Jewish temple. The Muslims built the Dome of the Rock there in 692.

Holy Land The name given by Christians to the area around Jerusalem and Bethlehem where Jesus lived and died. Muslims and Jews also call the region 'holy' for different reasons.

Holy Sepulchre The church in Jerusalem built over the site where, according to the Bible, Jesus was buried and was raised from the dead.

Iberia The region that we now know as Spain and Portugal. (See the map on pages 2–3.)

Indulgence A guarantee offered by the Latin Church. It promised sinners that their souls would pass straight to heaven after death without having to be cleansed by suffering in purgatory. Crusaders who kept their vows to free or defend Jerusalem were granted indulgences by the Pope.

Jihad A Muslim teaching meaning 'to strive' or 'struggle'. 'Greater jihad' requires all believers to struggle against sin in their own lives. 'Lesser jihad' is the struggle to defend Islam by war against non-believers, also known as Holy War.

Just War Christian teachings that defined the circumstances in which it was acceptable for Christians to engage in warfare.

Knights Minor nobles in western medieval society. A knight must be able to provide his own horse and weapons for fighting on horseback.

Knights of St John One of the Military Orders – men who took religious vows and served Christians by fighting to defend pilgrims and the Holy Land. Also known as the 'Hospitallers'.

Knights Templar One of the Military Orders – men who took religious vows and served Christians by fighting to defend pilgrims and the Holy Land.

Latin Church The Church of western Europe, based at Rome under the leadership of the Pope. Since the Middle Ages it has been known as the Roman Catholic Church.

Levant The name given to lands along the coast of the Near East with ports such as Tripoli and Acre. (See the map on page 3.)

Mamluks Ruling family of Muslims in Egypt from 1250 to 1517. They were originally slave-soldiers serving the caliphs of Egypt.

Mercenaries Soldiers who sell their skills for payment and fight in any cause for the rewards on offer.

Mesopotamia Land in the area we know today as Iraq.

Military Orders Soldier-monks such as the Knights Templar and the Knights of St John (Hospitallers).

Near East The region covering the lands at the eastern end of the Mediterranean Sea, for example, modern Greece, Turkey, Syria, Lebanon, Palestine, Israel and Egypt.

Night Journey The name given to the miraculous occasion when, according to Muslim belief, the Prophet Muhammad was taken up to heaven to learn directly from God how people should pray.

Orient Another word for the eastern world.

Ottoman Muslim Turkish tribe that grew to become the ruling power in Islam by the fifteenth century.

Outremer Name given by medieval western Europeans to the crusader states.

Pagans People who worship spirits rather than a single God. Medieval Christians sometimes wrongly called Muslims 'pagans'.

Palestine A region between Egypt and Syria in which the Holy Land is located.

Papacy The office of the Pope, leader of the Latin Church.

Papal bull A type of official letter or declaration made by the Pope.

Patriarch Title of a high ranking leader in the Christian Church, most often used in the Greek Church.

Penance Confessing sin and being granted forgiveness in return for doing certain acts to show a genuine desire for the cleansing of the soul.

Penitence/Penitential Acts such as fasting or going on pilgrimages to gain forgiveness for sins.

Piety Religious devotion and purity of life.

Pilgrimage A journey made for religious reasons.

Purgatory A place where, in the teaching of the Latin Church, those souls that will eventually go to heaven must spend time being cleansed (purged) by suffering before they can enter God's presence.

Reform An attempt to change and improve an organisation such as the Church Reform movement associated with Pope Gregory VII.

Regent A person who rules a kingdom until the rightful ruler is old enough or healthy enough to rule in his or her own strength.

Relic An object, such as an item of clothing or a body part, associated with a dead saint.

Sappers Soldiers who dug tunnels beneath walls and towers.

Saracens A name commonly used by westerners for Muslims in medieval times.

Seljuk Turks A tribe of recently converted Muslims that moved from central Asia into the Near East in the eleventh century.

Shi'ah One of the two main groups of Muslims, the other being Sunni. Shi'ites insist that the leadership of the Muslim world must pass down the family line of Prophet Muhammad.

Sufi Sufis are Muslims who emphasise the spiritual side of Islam through living a simple life without many material possessions and concentrate on getting closer to God.

Sultan The highest rank of Muslim ruler below the Caliph.

Sultanate of Rum The name given by Seljuk Turks to the lands they took in Anatolia from the Byzantine Christians.

Sunni One of the two main groups of Muslims, the other being Shi'ah. Sunni Muslims believe the leadership of the Muslim world should be held by those most suited to the role and leaders do not need to be descended from the Prophet Muhammad.

Syria Region in the Near East, between Palestine and Anatolia. (See the map on pages 2–3.)

Turks Tribes from central Asia who gradually moved eastwards into the Near East, particularly during the eleventh and twelfth centuries.

Index